WHISPERS
OF
WISDOM

WHISPERS OF WISDOM
IN PURSUIT OF *LAKSHMI*

R K SINGH

Published by
Renu Kaul Verma
Vitasta Publishing Pvt Ltd
4348/4C, Ansari Road, Daryaganj
New Delhi - 110 002
info@vitastapublishing.com

ISBN: 978-81-19670-22-2
© R K Singh
First Edition 2025
MRP ₹ 400

All Rights Reserved.
No part of this publication may be reproduced, stored in a retrieval system, or transmitted in any form, or by any means–electronic, mechanical, photocopying, recording or otherwise–without the prior permission of the publisher. Opinions expressed in this book are the author's own. The publisher is in no way responsible for these.

Edited by Priya Khanna
Illustrated by Bandana Paul
Typeset by Rohit Gautam
Cover Design by Shubhpreet Kaur
Printed by Manipal Technologies Limited, Manipal

जिंदगी पर एक किताब लिखेंगे
उसमें सारे हिसाब लिखेंगे
कुछ बदलते अपनों के लहजे
कुछ अपने टूटे ख्वाब लिखेंगे
कुछ अपने हालात लिखेंगे
उसमें ही सारी बात लिखेंगे
जो कह नही सकते वो सारे जज्बात लिखेंगे
ज़िन्दगी पर एक किताब लिखेंगे
उसमें सारे हिसाब लिखेंगे...

Contents

Foreword	*ix*
Between Home and the World	1
Of the Rulers and the Ruled	21
Expert Talk: Managing Your Finances and Business	33
In Pursuit of *Lakshmi:* Challenges and Conundrums	65
Around the world and a few Provocations	80
Chartered Accountancy	98
Words of Wisdom	106
The Tangled web of Bureaucracy	118
Movers and Shakers in my Life	121
The Last Word	130
A Word of Caution	136
Postscript	139
About the Author	*141*

Foreword

An invitation to my readers
Writing about oneself can sometimes tread a fine line between insightful reflection and narcissism. Leaders, celebrities, authors, and public figures often chronicle their lives with a sense of authority, underpinned by the belief that their experience will hold the public's interest.

However, the impulse to share one's personal journey isn't reserved solely for the well-known or influential. Why then, should someone like me, who is not particularly famous, choose to document my experiences for others to read and reflect upon? This book begins with this premise.

My motivation to pen down my memoirs springs from a desire to bridge the temporal divide, to connect the past with the present, and inform the future. It is about leaving a legacy that outlasts the ephemeral rush of our daily lives—a legacy that offers the next generation a glimpse into a time when life wasn't perpetually rushed, and the texture of everyday existence was markedly different. Through these pages, I aim to provide a navigational chart of sorts, guiding future generations through the lessons learned from my own life, thus sparing them the currency of time and effort.

From the earliest days of my youth, I harboured ambitions of becoming an industrialist and was eager to introduce innovative concepts and designs to the marketplace. This vision was underpinned by a commitment to excellence, innovation, and creativity, driven by a worldview that prizes progress and the advancement of society. My life has been inextricably linked with this mission, consistently prioritising personal relationships and family over professional recognition or material success.

Indeed, my greatest achievements have not been graced with public accolades, but rather embodied by a life lived with purpose and engagement. I have savoured the finest cuisines, journeyed widely, and embraced knowledge from every corner of my environment.

I've been a pillar of support to those in my circle, extending support to allies and critics alike, driven by a spirit of altruism rather than with the anticipation of recompense.

Nevertheless, my journey has not been devoid of shortcomings. My stint in Mumbai, for instance, fell short of yielding the business triumphs I had envisioned, and despite my earnest endeavours, I never quite reached the heights of becoming the celebrated industrialist of my dreams.

Moreover, as a fervent nationalist, it pains me to acknowledge that I have yet to witness India overcome the external adversities I've long fought against. Yet, I remain hopeful that with more time, I can still contribute significantly to these goals, pushing forward both my personal ambitions and the broader objectives of my nation.

Through the vivid chapters of my life—from the untainted innocence of childhood and the numerous trials of adulthood, to the reflective years of senior citizenship—life has unfurled a rich mosaic of experiences. These experiences have profoundly shaped my understanding across a spectrum of social, professional, and personal dimensions. Beyond the structured learning of academia, life's greatest lessons have come from a tapestry of subtle interactions and impactful realisations.

In this memoir, I recount the journey of my life, a narrative that stretches over 59.5 years. This odyssey has witnessed a progression from a simplistic grasp of the world to a more layered and broadened perspective, enriched by a multitude of experiences that have significantly shaped my perceptions and beliefs. Through these pages, I invite you, the reader, to traverse this journey with me, exploring the contours of a life lived fully, with its triumphs and tribulations, in the hope that it might offer insights, inspiration, and perhaps a roadmap for your own path.

Documenting challenges

Documenting the rich tapestry of human experience without bias or partiality poses a significant challenge in an age where sensitivity and political correctness are paramount. As a society, we strive to avoid offending, yet we are easily aggrieved. The colourful array of identities that define us cannot be ignored, as their omission would render any account of human experiences uninspiringly uniform. Keeping this in mind, I have chosen to omit specific names, castes, or religious affiliations in my memoir to ensure the broadest possible resonance and applicability.

This decision aims to allow readers from diverse

backgrounds to see reflections of their own journeys in these pages, without the distraction of potentially divisive details. Additionally, I have carefully curated and sometimes subtly modified certain experiences to mitigate a natural inclination toward envy or resentment. This editorial approach is deliberate, designed to cultivate a narrative that fosters empathy and understanding, rather than discord.

Throughout this book, I recount numerous moments of gratitude and acknowledge those who have enriched my life's journey, though some acknowledgments are too profound for mere words to capture adequately.

I am particularly grateful to Shri Anil Maheshwari, whose encouragement and insightful guidance were crucial in transforming my scattered reflections into a coherent and published memoir. His advocacy for authenticity over preaching has deeply influenced the spirit of this work. I must also thank my doctor, professor and surgeon, Dr K N Shrivastava, for his recommendation of ten-days' rest, which provided a precious pause for deep introspection and writing. This restful period, a stark contrast to the isolation of the pandemic lockdown, offered a peaceful interlude to ponder the intricate and sometimes poignant moments of my life.

This book aims to leave a legacy of insights that could provide guidance and wisdom to others as they navigate the complexities of their social and professional environments. It is designed to enrich and inform, assisting future generations in confronting similar challenges and celebrating similar triumphs.

I extend my deepest gratitude to everyone who has influenced my life, each contributing to the intricate mosaic of experiences that have shaped my perspective.

To all who have participated in this journey, through its highs and lows, I offer my heartfelt thanks. Your involvement has been crucial, and I cherish every lesson along the path we have shared.

In grappling with the idealism that often complicates our lives, I have come to view it as both a necessary impulse and a potential hindrance. While idealism can inspire and drive progress, it must be tempered with pragmatism to prevent it from overshadowing the practical aspects of living. Our lives, so ordinary in their rhythms and routines, are nevertheless complete. Embracing self-love and personal contentment is paramount; we must prioritise our well-being to effectively share our best selves with others.

By sharing these reflections, I aim to highlight the intricate weave of personal and professional life, suggesting that true success and fulfilment arise from a blend of ambition, ethical living, and a commitment to making a positive impact. As you, the reader, embark on this narrative journey, you will encounter the unvarnished truths of a life perhaps not unlike your own. In sharing these stories, I hope to connect with you on a fundamental level, discovering common ground in our shared experiences, challenges, and triumphs. Let us delve into this narrative together, exploring from the very beginning the realities that bind us as a community and as individuals in a complex world.

Between Home and the World

My life's journey began in a vibrant district headquarters town, characterised by the colourful contrast between bustling city life and the tranquil rural experiences of my parents' village in a neighbouring district. These early years laid the foundation for a life filled with rich, diverse encounters that have been both formative and enlightening.

As an adult, I expanded my horizons and moved to the National Capital Region (NCR), a decision that propelled me into new educational and professional realms, yet I found myself frequently returning to my hometown—a picturesque town nestled in the Shivalik foothills, renowned for its vibrant spirit and a touch of rebelliousness.

My childhood memories are largely joyful and vivid, marked by community interactions and playful adventures. However, one incident stands out distinctly, offering a blend of suspense and life lessons.

At the tender age of three, alongside my slightly younger brother, I embarked on an unintended adventure that led us far from home. This misadventure spurred a frantic search by our neighbours, ultimately culminating in our rescue by a kind-hearted rickshaw driver. His selflessness not only brought relief but also taught me about the value of community support and the kindness of strangers. This episode, lasting over four tension-filled hours, fortified my resilience and instilled a profound confidence in exploring new environments, secure in the belief that I could always find my way back.

Despite the warmth of most childhood memories, not all were as pleasant. A particularly striking memory involves an unjust reprimand at the age of six, delivered by a local police inspector influenced by a trivial complaint from his granddaughter over a minor squabble during play. This encounter with authority at such a young age opened my eyes to the complexities of community dynamics and the imperfections of the justice system, imprinting on me the importance of fairness and the need for reform within the police force.

Our neighbourhood was also the setting for less than desirable interactions, particularly with a nosy neighbour whose intrusive tendencies disrupted our communal harmony. Her penchant for meddling in the private affairs of residents brought unnecessary tension and discomfort, contrasting sharply with the otherwise tight-knit community spirit.

On the flip side, the neighbourhood also housed figures who brought warmth and wisdom, such as a retired railway official who became a beloved storyteller among the children. His narratives about the era of British rule were not only engaging but also educational, imparting lessons on integrity and honesty that went beyond the classroom. His interactions bridged the gap between generations, enriching our young minds with historical insights and moral values, and knitting the community closer together.

This rich tapestry of experiences from my childhood through to my adult life in the NCR has been a profound journey of learning, growth, and personal development. The stark contrast between the nurturing, yet occasionally challenging, environment of my hometown and the dynamic, fast-paced life in the NCR have provided me with a unique perspective on life.

As I ventured into my educational and professional endeavours in the NCR, the lessons learned from the community and the values instilled by figures, like the retired railway official, continued to influence me profoundly.

These narratives, rich with historical anecdotes and life lessons, are not merely recollections; they are a celebration of the human spirit, a testament to the resilience of community bonds, and a call to appreciate the intricate blend of relationships that shape our lives. As we navigate through our days, these stories remind us of the importance of community, the value of our roots, and the enduring impact of history on our personal and collective identities.

The contrasting social fabric of my paternal and maternal villages offered a vivid tableau of rural life, each marked by its unique character and cultural nuances. My paternal village was populated by dynamic individuals predominantly focused on agricultural productivity and local craftsmanship.

Despite the absence of significant vices such as gambling or alcoholism, the community was not without its flaws, as subtle currents of jealousy and resentment often undercut it. This undercurrent sometimes manifested in petty disputes and a quiet competitiveness, which occasionally overshadowed the village's many virtues.

In stark contrast, my maternal village presented a more complex mosaic. Though it grappled with more conspicuous vices, it was also a place of profound communal warmth and vibrant traditions. One of my most cherished memories involves exchanging homemade ice cream for grain—a simple barter practice that brought immense joy and delicious flavours that linger in my memory. Additionally, my grandmother's tender care for her cows illuminated the deep, almost sacred connections between humans and animals in village life, teaching me lessons about empathy, stewardship, and the interdependence of life.

Amidst these pastoral settings, some of my formative experiences occurred in the workshops of a local goldsmith and a carpenter, whom I affectionately called *nana*. These artisans mastered their crafts and embodied the ethical and aesthetic values that defined true artisanship.

The goldsmith's workshop was a realm of transformation where precious metals and stones were meticulously crafted into beautiful artefacts. Each piece bore the imprint of his dedication and precision, turning simple materials into treasures of great worth and beauty.

Similarly, the carpenter's workshop was a sanctuary of creation. The scent of freshly cut wood and the sound of the saw and chisel rhythmically shaping the wood remain vivid in my memory. He taught me that each stroke was an intentional act of creation and that patience and meticulous care could imbue even the most straightforward piece of timber with elegance and purpose. Through these experiences, I understood that craftsmanship is not merely about the skills one employs but also about the integrity and respect one brings to the work. It is about transforming raw elements with a reverence for the craft and a commitment to contributing lasting value to the world.

Reflecting on the tapestry of my childhood evokes a vivid panorama of life in a neighbourhood that was a melting pot of contrasting lives—from esteemed doctors and lawyers to government employees, alongside a smattering of unabashed vagabonds.

Despite occasional skirmishes that sometimes escalated to the sound of gunfire, there was an undeniable charm to our communal life. The temple ground, a hub of youthful exuberance, doubled as a playground, while its vicinity served as a gathering spot for card games and morning exercises at the local Rashtriya Swayamsevak Sangh (RSS) *shakhas*, drawing participation from many.

A sacred *peepal* tree and a *neem* tree stood as pillars of our community's spiritual and health practices. Women and elders revered the peepal tree for worship, and the neem tree was cherished for its medicinal virtues, providing natural toothpaste and remedies for various ailments. The daily rhythm was punctuated by early morning calls from the temple and the mosque, signalling the start of each day.

Our local dynamics were especially animated by the youth, many of whom, caught in the throes of adolescence, seemed more inclined to wield weapons than books.

The markets—a bustling scene of trade—often marked the boundaries of Hindu and Muslim neighbourhoods and were frequent flashpoints during communal unrest. Yet, this volatile backdrop was paradoxically a setting for a stronger civic sense than today, characterised by a deep respect for elders, women, and communal care for children.

Travel to the paternal village was always an adventure filled with anticipation. Securing a window seat on the bus, engaging with vendors, and observing the notably kinder conduct of bus drivers and conductors compared to those in Delhi, were part of the journey's thrill. Upon arrival, the village shop served as a makeshift shelter where the allure of freshly made *ladoos* beckoned. Our walk home was punctuated with respectful greetings to elders, resonating through the village air.

Our family *haveli* was a microcosm of village life, complete with a Neem tree that provided both shade and entertainment. The aromas of cooking from nearby kitchens, the sight of milk frothing in pots, and the communal spaces where villagers gathered to rest, discuss daily matters, or smoke *hookahs* in the evenings painted a picture of a closely-knit community.

Our agricultural lands, scattered across different locales, were accessible by bullock-cart—a mode of transport that offered its own rustic charm compared to tractors. The surrounding greenery, fruit-bearing trees, and the diverse avian life added layers of beauty and tranquillity to our rural life.

Seasonal festivals like *Holi* and the annual *Naumi* fair were the highlights of the year, featuring dramatisations of epic tales and a plethora of cinema, theatre, foods, and crafts that drew crowds from across the region. Community-driven efforts ensured village cleanliness and harmony, making each communal gathering a cherished memory.

The quality and taste of food in the village, now seemingly unparalleled even by five-star standards, spoke of a time when the integrity of ingredients played a crucial role in culinary delights. Adventures while riding on horse carts or the thrill of driving in an overcrowded tempo added to the mosaic of my childhood memories.

The village hosts its first barter Olympics

Visits to the maternal village brought different joys, such as train rides, during which my siblings and I would engage in a playful renaming of stations and listen intently to the cadences of vendors' calls. The village fairs, walks along train tracks, and the playful tradition of placing coins on rails to see them flattened by passing trains, were adventures that defined our days.

These reflections are not just the recollections of a simpler time; they form a narrative of a life enriched by community, tradition, and the simple joys of rural India. They underscore the essence of growing up in an environment where every individual, every tree, and every building had a role in the communal tapestry, fostering a sense of belonging and shared heritage that I carry with me to this day.

My schooling

My childhood unfolded in a neighbourhood that was a crucible of contrasts—home to diverse professions and characters, from doctors and advocates to traders and government employees, juxtaposed with elements of lawlessness that often stifled personal growth and community cohesion. The reality of my upbringing was not just about community spirit and playful childhood escapades; it was also shadowed by the undercurrents of crime and local dominance.

Donation drives, frequently cloaked in the guise of religious or community welfare, often served more sinister purposes. One particularly stark memory involves a poor postman who, having refused to contribute to a Holi donation, found his doors forcibly removed and burned in the ceremonial Holi fire. This act of intimidation was a clear message of the power dynamics at play.

In another instance, a family that could not afford substantial donations suffered greatly; their daughters became targets of harassment, illustrating the brutal consequences of failing to comply with imposed 'contributions' and highlighting the deep-seated corruption that could pervade even the most mundane aspects of daily life.

School life mirrored these community challenges, marked by its own set of adversities. From classes six to eight, I faced the wrath of a science teacher who resented my academic success—perhaps a reflection of his own personal frustrations with his sons' academic performances. This teacher's antagonism only fuelled my determination, and I excelled, notably topping the school in class eight. In a mix of celebration and defiance, I used my scholarship money to buy sweets for the teaching staff, a gesture that served both as a celebration of my achievements and a subtle critique of their unfair treatment.

The negative experiences at school influenced my educational choices profoundly. By class nine, driven by rumours of problematic teachers in the science track, I switched to commerce. This shift brought new challenges; my commerce teacher discouraged my practice of completing the accounting homework in English, which I did as I was aiming to prepare for my future academic requirements in an English medium school. Despite not yielding to the pressure to take private tuition from him, I managed to secure the second position in the class.

In class ten, the pressure intensified with a math teacher who insisted I take private tuition from him. I resisted and instead sought help from an English teacher who eventually agreed to tutor me in math just four months before the board exams. His support was pivotal in helping me not only to pass the exams, but to also secure a national scholarship, further defying the low expectations some teachers held for me.

Additionally, my class nine year was complicated by a Hindi teacher who turned a blind eye to rampant cheating during exams—a practice from which I and a few other ethically minded students abstained. Fortunately, I was bolstered by a strong peer group, including several academically gifted students who had pursued the science subjects.

The high school I attended was recognised for its rigorous discipline, contributing significantly to its academic successes. Yet, it lacked a commerce stream, leading me and several fellow students to advocate for its inclusion. Despite months of campaigning and numerous letters to the Chief Minister, it took a year for the school to introduce commerce, prompting me to transfer to an older Gujarati school in the interim.

This new educational setting presented a drastic change; it was dominated by unruly students and unsupportive teachers, save for an exceptional economics teacher who was unfortunately marginalised by the administration. My time there was fraught with challenges, from navigating clerical corruption to contending with unfairly biased grading practices.

These formative years in education left an indelible mark on my understanding of social and academic integrity, exposing the systemic issues prevalent within our schooling systems. As I navigated these environments, I learned critical lessons about resilience, integrity, and self-advocacy, which have informed my broader perspective on the need for substantive educational reforms.

Addressing the culture of bullying and intimidation that permeates many aspects of life is crucial. By confronting

Refusal of donation leads to bullies breaking and burning the house front door

and mitigating these issues, we can foster a society that is more ethical, innovative, and inclusive—a society where individuals are empowered to thrive without fear of reprisal for non-conformity.

Over the last fifty years, I have observed a marked decline in the rich tapestry of craftsmanship and the deep connection with nature that once epitomised village life. The communal spaces where skills were shared and accomplishments celebrated have slowly eroded, overshadowed by the relentless march of modernity.

While technological advancements have brought many benefits, they have also precipitated a disconnection from age-old practices and a sustainable way of life, contributing to a noticeable degradation in both the quality of life and the preservation of cultural values centred around craftsmanship.

As we face pressing environmental and social challenges today, it becomes increasingly important to revisit and revitalise these ancestral traditions. There is a compelling need to rekindle the traditional practices that once fostered sustainable living and community bonding. By doing so, we can forge a path towards a more sustainable and interconnected existence that respects both our heritage and the natural world.

Reflecting on simpler times, the long rusk and sweet buns from our neighbourhood bakery, run by the beloved nanaji, remain etched in my memory as symbols of my childhood's culinary joys. More than their delightful taste, it was nanaji's heartfelt warmth and generosity that made those treats so special. Each visit to his bakery was not just a transaction but an exchange of kindness, making every bite of those buns taste of nostalgia and warmth.

Contrasting sharply with these sweet memories are my

interactions with the local children during my visits to the village. Raised in an urban setting, my siblings and I were always viewed as outsiders. Our different ways of speaking, dressing, and behaving marked us out as different, erecting invisible walls that were hard to cross. These barriers necessitated a constant effort on our part to integrate, making every playtime a delicate dance of negotiation and adaptation.

The village playground was a microcosm of the broader social challenges we faced—spaces where belonging had to be continually earned and where our identities were both a barrier and a bridge. These experiences, though fraught with tension, were invaluable lessons in adaptability and resilience, teaching us how to navigate and embrace diverse social landscapes without losing our sense of self.

Each visit to the paternal village reawakened my culinary passions, particularly for the traditional *mawa ladoos* and *rabri*, which were prepared with recipes handed down through generations. These dishes were not merely treats but were threads that connected me to my familial past, their rich flavours and creamy textures reviving my connection to a heritage that valued deep and meaningful culinary practices.

These reflections are not merely reminiscences but are a call to recognise and preserve the fading arts of culinary mastery and communal living. They underscore a broader narrative of preserving cultural legacies and fostering an environment where modern advancements complement rather than supplant traditional wisdom.

Myth of an idyllic village

In the village, interactions among the children were often subdued; there were neither profound friendships nor deep-seated animosities. It was a portrait of everyday normalcy, where residents mastered the art of living together while maintaining individual boundaries. Our engagements were marked by a polite distance—a courteous but detached manner that was starkly different from the more intricate and sometimes tense relations among the adults. Our periodic visits from the city painted us as novelties, regarded with both curiosity and reservation. Nevertheless, some warm-hearted locals consistently fostered friendly ties with us, bridging the gaps that might have otherwise isolated us.

One of the cultural pillars of village life was the annual Naumi fair, a festive event that extended beyond mere entertainment to celebrate local culinary arts and crafts. The fair was animated by the irresistible aroma of *jalebis*—golden, syrup-soaked spirals of fried dough that drew crowds from across the village. Additionally, the village was renowned for its traditional mud-roasted *handi* and the uniquely delectable *saag*—a rich concoction of black lentils and spinach rice that offered a culinary experience unmatched even by high-end gastronomic establishments like ITC Maurya's restaurant, Bukhara.

These experiences collectively painted a vibrant tapestry of village life, replete with rich culinary traditions and complex social dynamics that profoundly shaped my appreciation for the delicate balance between tradition and personal identity.

During my youth, working in the fields until the age of 18, I cultivated a deep respect for agriculture, recognising it as both an art and a science that could dramatically boost productivity and improve the villagers' economic conditions.

Despite the introduction of technological advancements and increased financial flows in the post-1990 era, these changes often failed to preserve the core traditional practices and sustainable methods that were integral to village life. Rather than bridging old and new ways, the influx of modernity sometimes caused a rift, leading to a gradual erosion of the village's lush vibrancy and a departure from the harmonious rhythms that had long been in tune with nature.

Between bullying and getting bullied
From my childhood, I have observed the widespread prevalence of bullying, which spans environments from quaint villages to bustling metropolitan areas. My personal encounters with this destructive behaviour extended from neighbourhood *mohallas* to affluent colonies and across educational institutions from primary schools to colleges. This troubling culture is not confined to educational settings but pervades government offices and corporate workplaces, where a desire to dominate disrupts the focus and peace of diligent students and professionals.

Shockingly, this bullying is evident even among high-ranking officers in the Indian Administrative Services (IAS) and the Indian Police Service (IPS), who often dominate other government service personnel. This is compounded by trade unions that are politically backed and who frequently intimidate officers. This atmosphere results in a scarcity of skilled labour, ethical professionalism, and competent management, severely stifling innovation and the development of new products, processes, medicines, machinery, and software.

Politically, the bullying culture infiltrates the electoral processes. In elections for assemblies and parliaments, it is not the general populace but influential families and their cliques that sway outcomes, bullying the public into submission and hindering the formation of independent, informed opinions. This systemic intimidation stifles genuine democratic engagement and perpetuates political disenfranchisement.

To address these pervasive issues, it is crucial to foster a cultural shift within law enforcement and governance, transitioning from a paradigm of domination and intimidation to one emphasising respect, civility, and service. This shift involves training and empowering individuals in authority to facilitate community and professional growth, fostering an environment where respect and constructive interaction are paramount.

Over the past five decades, I have witnessed the challenges that villages face in harmonising modernity with their natural environment. Despite the introduction of modern conveniences designed to simplify life, these advancements often lead village life away from its harmonious coexistence with nature. This global challenge is transforming not only the physical landscape but also the cultural and social fabric, making it increasingly difficult to preserve the sustainable and community-oriented lifestyle that once defined rural living.

The transformation becomes starkly evident during the village's Holi festival, traditionally a vibrant celebration of community unity featuring colourful theatrical performances over ten days. This festival used to unify the community in a spirit that rivalled the allure of cinematic entertainment. However, increasing political awareness and the influence of partisan politics have marred this cherished event, turning it into a source of conflict, diminishing communal joy, and detracting from the cultural storytelling that once defined it.

The excessive political consciousness has notably reduced India's charm, contributing to a decline in practical skills and fostering a culture marked by animosity. The once-prevalent communal harmony and adeptness have given way to a culture of shouting and disrespect, even toward elders, representing a significant departure from the traditional values of respect and civility.

These issues resonate within the NCR, where the local atmosphere is often marked by arrogance and a distinct lack of communal unity. Common disputes, such as those over parking and one-upmanship, highlight the ongoing contentions in this area. This urban environment contrasts starkly with the ethos of rural areas, which could potentially foster a more cohesive community life if they were better equipped with essential civic amenities. However, urban settings frequently attract residents out of necessity rather than preference, resulting in neighbourhoods populated by 'compulsive inhabitants' rather than harmoniously integrated communities.

This dichotomy between urban and rural experiences highlights the need for thoughtful urban planning and community development that fosters genuine social cohesion and respects the delicate balance between modernity and tradition.

What really changed?

Remarkably, I have observed that people living farther apart often maintain better relationships than those living in close proximity. This phenomenon might be attributed to the psychological space that distance affords, allowing individuals to deeply appreciate and value their interactions. Over the past thirty-five years, a suburb of Delhi, once renowned for its rich civic culture, has experienced a disturbing shift towards disorder, with only a handful of exceptions preserving the area's original character. Despite being one of the significant towns established post-independence, the focus of government and influential individuals on rapid, often unstructured, infrastructure development has largely neglected the creation of a cohesive township culture. The lack of essential civic structures like a town hall or an assembly square, crucial for fostering community engagement and effective governance, is particularly alarming and indicative of a broader systemic neglect.

Furthermore, the local governance structure appears stagnant, with a noticeable absence of elected representatives in villages such as panchayats and municipalities, reflecting a concerning disinterest from political and administrative bodies. Despite nearing its fiftieth anniversary, this city still seems mired in a developmental limbo, perpetually on the brink of progress yet failing to achieve a stable, mature status as a fully developed community.

The emergence of Residential Welfare Associations (RWAs) represents a concerted effort to address these governance shortcomings. However, while these organisations strive to resolve community issues, they often inadvertently mirror the inefficiencies of broader governmental structures, introducing an additional layer of bureaucracy. This not only complicates the governance landscape but also shifts responsibility from central government institutions to localised bodies. While such decentralisation is crucial, it highlights the ongoing challenges in maintaining effective democratic governance and ensuring accountability at all levels.

Reflecting on my diverse experiences, from village life to urban settings, it is evident that the environments we inhabit, and the governance structures that shape them, profoundly

In future, meetings will be held outdoors

impact our lives. As we navigate these complex social landscapes, the critical need to foster a sense of community and restore efficient governance becomes increasingly apparent. These are vital steps toward cultivating a more harmonious and integrated society.

The shift from a community-focused to a more fragmented and contentious society underscores deep-seated challenges in urban planning, governance, and social values. Addressing these issues requires thoughtful analysis and proactive strategies. By creating a balanced, well-planned urban environment with active, engaged local governance, we can rejuvenate community spirit and ensure that cities and suburbs alike can flourish as cohesive, vibrant communities.

Of the Rulers and the Ruled

My interactions with governance as an ordinary citizen oscillate between frustration, disillusionment, and fleeting moments of hope. I often feel like a minor component in a vast machinery ostensibly designed to serve me but frequently functioning contrary to my needs.

On one side, there are politicians with their unfulfilled promises to their voters and on the other side are the bureaucrats, who are more inclined towards preserving the status quo than genuinely aiding the populace. The system appears tailored to shield those in power rather than to address the needs of the common folk.

Navigating the byzantine structures of government agencies often involves battling through a morass of paperwork, enduring long queues, and dealing with indifferent officials who seem to take perverse pleasure in uttering 'no' or 'come back later.' It feels as if they are using a deliberately arcane and daunting language.

Yet, amidst these challenges, there are rays of hope—

public servants dedicated to their roles, tirelessly working behind the scenes, often unrecognised and unrewarded. These individuals renew my belief that perhaps the system can indeed be bettered. However, my overarching sentiment toward governance is one of disillusionment, punctuated by persistent quests for hope, where my voice seems drowned out by special interests and backroom decisions.

As I continue to speak out, vote, and hold leaders accountable, I support those who envision a better future and strive towards a governance system that genuinely serves its citizens. But let us begin at the start. Have we effectively distanced ourselves from the legacy of the British Raj?

The British monarchy, enduring over a millennium, exemplifies a successful model wielding global influence both overtly and subtly. The UK maintains a prominent international role via platforms like the United Nations (UN) and the Commonwealth. Its influence extends through myriad treaties and collaborations, positioning it as a significant global player despite its monarchical system, celebrated for its robust democracy. This is highlighted by an exemplary police force, disaster response teams, and governance in domains such as space and maritime.

Notably, the election of prime ministers from minority or non-white backgrounds in Britain illustrates the inclusivity of British democratic values, a profound statement, given its history of colonial rule over diverse populations.

Contrasting this with my personal experiences of governance at home paints a different picture. From 1974 to 1980, I recall an efficient system where issues with utilities were promptly resolved with just a signature on a complaint form. Today, this responsiveness has waned, replaced by apathy and inertia, indicative of a decline in governmental duty and accountability. Despite greater resources and technological advances, there is a stark decline in service delivery.

Moreover, the link between population growth and the availability of civic amenities is not as straightforward as often portrayed. While population increases are frequently blamed for resource depletion, inadequate planning and management are likely more culpable. Effective governance hinges not on population control but on improving the system's efficiency and accountability to better serve the growing population.

Examples and more examples

When I was a student living in a small flat, I faced a dangerous situation due to a short circuit caused by a government-installed cable. This forced me to rig a temporary solution to maintain the electricity supply during exams. However, when we reported this safety hazard, instead of a prompt and understanding response, the response from the Subdivision Officer (SDO)—notoriously known for his corrupt practices—was disheartening. Rather than addressing the critical issue, he launched an investigation, and his associate visited the flat with threats of severe penalties and imprisonment for our makeshift electrical setup.

For three gruelling days, I was ensnared in bureaucratic red tape, deprived of electricity, and met with hostility instead of assistance. It was only through connections with higher officials that my plight was eventually resolved. This ordeal was a stark lesson in the reality of governmental inefficiencies and the critical importance of having connections to access basic public services—contrary to the principles of justice and equality that should underlie all public service.

This experience is indicative of a broader issue—a disconnect between the ideals of public service and the practical reality, both internationally and within nations over time. It emphasises the need for a rigorous reassessment of governmental structures and functions, their accountability, and the integrity and efficacy with which they perform their civic duties.

Elaborating on contemporary challenges and makeshift solutions in utilities and services, I find that in many urban households, individuals resort to installing personal submersible pumps for groundwater access and rely on Reverse Osmosis (RO) systems or bottled water for drinking, given the unreliable municipal supply. However, the safety and health standards of these stopgap solutions, particularly bottled water, remain under-regulated, raising concerns about their safety and efficacy.

The unreliable electricity grid has pushed many to adopt alternative power sources such as generators, inverters, and solar panels. These alternatives not only provide backup during outages but also grant a measure of independence from conventional power sources. Solar energy presents a sustainable choice that could lessen both environmental impact and long-term energy costs.

The privatisation of healthcare has transformed hospitals into establishments mirroring five-star hotels, prioritising luxury over essential care, with minimal regulatory oversight over pricing. This transformation is compounded by an opaque system of referral kickbacks among doctors, pharmaceutical companies, and diagnostic centres, inflating the cost of medical care without enhancing the quality of service.

Moreover, the police force, traditionally tasked with

community protection, now often places the onus of security on the citizens themselves, urging them to take measures like hiring private security or installing surveillance systems. The decline of community-based policing, such as the beat constable system, has eroded public trust and diminished the effectiveness of public safety services.

However, amidst these challenges, there are beacons of hope, such as a recent encounter with a dedicated surgeon whose ethical practice and patient-centric approach provided not only excellent medical results but also restored faith in a healthcare system often criticised for its commercialisation. Such experiences underscore the potential for professionalism and compassion within the medical field, highlighting the critical role of integrity and patient-first values in healthcare.

These scenarios underscore a social shift towards privatisation and individual initiative in securing basic services, driven by both technological advances and failures in public governance. While private solutions may offer immediate benefits, they also raise significant questions about sustainability, equity, and the fundamental responsibilities of the government in ensuring access to essential human needs.

Addressing quality in basic necessities

Adulteration and compromised quality in daily essentials such as milk, medicine, cooking oils, spices, and even fruits and vegetables, pose significant challenges that undermine a nation's health and economic integrity. True progress is not measured solely by the ability to construct imposing structures of cement, steel, and technology. Rather, genuine development is gauged by the consistent provision of high-quality and affordable food, education, and healthcare—

the foundations for nurturing a healthy, educated, and productive populace. Overlooking these basics in favour of large-scale infrastructure can cultivate an environment ripe for exploitation and corruption, driven by unchecked greed.

Consider our local milkman's situation, which illustrates the broader issue. He initially claimed that he only added water to milk. Over time, pressured by market realities, he admitted that over 75 per cent of the milk he sold was artificially synthesised, making it financially unfeasible for him to sell pure milk without hiking prices to cover the costs of maintaining and transporting buffalos. Consequently, we stopped purchasing from him, a scenario reminiscent of losing access to authentic products once common in our youth.

Similarly, the widespread adulteration affecting oils, ghee, and produce shifts standards far from natural cultivation, making original flavours and health benefits increasingly rare. Yet, this issue seldom stirs government action or public outcry in the world's largest democracy, indicating a disconnect between the populace and their representatives and a decline in community advocacy.

This narrative extends into professional ethics across various sectors. I remember a doctor from my childhood village who, lacking proper qualifications, treated both humans and animals by borrowing credibility from his brother, a veterinary doctor. This situation points to broader issues in rural healthcare standards, where underqualified practitioners often serve vulnerable populations, placing them at risk.

In 1995, I encountered a doctor in a remote village's Primary Health Centre who seldom visited his place of posting, yet drew a full salary, illustrating systemic flaws in healthcare access and quality. In contrast, a qualified MBBS doctor in my neighbourhood struggled to attract enough patients to sustain his practice, while less qualified practitioners enjoyed steady patronage. This misalignment underscores the need for stricter regulatory oversight and public education to maintain medical standards.

Without a steadfast commitment to improving the quality and integrity of essential services and goods, nations risk perpetuating cycles of poor health, educational deficits, and economic stagnation. Only through concerted efforts to enhance professional standards, ensure product quality, and engage an informed citizenry can we aspire to meet the criteria for a truly developed and content society.

As for public transportation, my shift from buses and trains to private vehicles was driven by a desire to avoid the increasing civic disorder pervasive in these settings. Once domains of shared experiences and mutual respect, public spaces have become arenas of frustration marked by frequent disrespect and discord, making them less appealing.

Despite these trials, travel—especially by train—has offered enriching experiences and profound human connections. Engaging with seasoned travellers has provided valuable life lessons, and acts of kindness during journeys have reinforced the importance of compassion in communal settings.

My international travels have widened my perspective, exposing me to superior standards in human capital management, citizen behaviour, and professional conduct. These experiences underscore the stark differences in how societies manage public spaces and highlight the potential for substantial improvements in my home country.

Through these reflections, I emphasise that while economic growth is essential, it should proceed together with advances in civic education and public decorum to truly transform society into one that is as prosperous as it is gracious and well-mannered.

Travels and encounters with more rules
During one of my travels abroad, I found myself transitioning between cities in a foreign land. During a short layover, I attempted to purchase coffee and snacks, only to discover that I did not have the local currency, baht, and the vendor's credit card machine was malfunctioning.

Despite my offer to pay in dollars, the vendor, bound by his limitations, could not accept. None of my companions offered to assist, but our guide stepped in, covering the cost. Later, when I tried to repay him after exchanging my money, he graciously declined, emphasising that the cost was minimal and, as I was a guest in his country, he was happy to cover it. He expressed that he earned his living by his profession, not by capitalising on acts of kindness, reminding me of the integrity I encountered with a guide in Greece who resisted exploiting financial opportunities despite economic hardships in his country.

In Dubai, while I encountered neither particularly positive nor negative personal interactions, the city's architectural grandeur and operational efficiency left a profound impression. This experience contrasted starkly with the less organised infrastructure back home, highlighting significant disparities in urban planning and management.

A subsequent 10-day visit to China exposed me to a society that adheres rigidly to systems, maintaining cleanliness and demonstrating effective macro-management. Discussions revealed that countries adhering to Standard

Operating Procedures (SOPs) from western nations often excel in civic management, a lesson in the importance of structured governance systems for maintaining public order and cleanliness.

In my own country, at religious sites like Maharashtra's bustling Sai temple and Amritsar's Golden temple, I witnessed affluent Sikhs volunteering for menial services, which profoundly illustrated how community leaders can foster a strong civic sense among followers.

Reflecting on these experiences, I advocate for global hospitality standards that treat travellers with respect and kindness, rather than viewing them as easy targets. This approach should extend to service industries and law enforcement, emphasising civility and service over exploitation and dominance. For example, introducing mandatory civility training for commercial drivers could significantly enhance both tourist and local experiences.

Moreover, the culture of service that I have observed abroad, contrasts starkly with the entitlement often seen in domestic settings, where the focus is more on claiming rights than on fulfilling duties. These reflections highlight the need for substantial reforms across various public sectors to promote a more welcoming and respectful social ethos.

This journey has not only enriched my understanding of global standards but also underscored the crucial interplay between efficient governance and quality of life, reminding us that true progress is holistic and inclusive, demanding both structural and cultural shifts to foster a genuinely advanced society.

The Bureaucracy and the judiciary: Have you heard?

Throughout my sixteen-year tenure in the public sector, I have observed that our bureaucracy often seems designed more for fostering mediocrity than meritocracy. Young, talented individuals enter the system with high aspirations, only to find themselves stifled by an environment that promotes complacency over innovation. This culture not only inhibits personal growth but also diminishes the overall effectiveness of public service.

The situation can be likened to the work of carpenters: while a skilled carpenter can create beautiful furniture from average wood, an inept one can ruin even the finest materials. Sadly, in my experience across both public and private sectors, I have often witnessed the dismantling of good systems and the marginalisation of those who strive to maintain high standards. This disregard for excellence and discipline, unfortunately, extends beyond the workplace and permeates everyday life.

For instance, during my travels abroad, I was struck by the disciplined behaviour in public spaces—there was no unnecessary honking, and people patiently queued in shops, contrasting starkly with the behaviour often displayed in my country. This lack of civic discipline seems driven by a social attitude that equates rowdiness with power, undermining the very fabric of community and respect.

Upon witnessing effective waste management and cleaning systems overseas, I initially thought our government was indifferent to such responsibilities. However, I later realised that the issue is not solely with governance but also with a social ethos that does not prioritise cleanliness or order. The phrase *achcha dikho* (look good) should be more than a slogan;

it should be a rallying call for maintaining cleanliness and civic decorum as part of broader initiatives like the *Swachh Bharat* (Clean India) campaign.

From an early age, I learned that knowledge can turn those around you into adversaries, especially when they are unwilling or unable to understand or embrace what you know. This was clear even during my school days. Despite excelling academically, one teacher opposed promoting me, citing financial implications for the school—a blatant display of injustice that forced me to transfer to another school where I faced similar challenges.

These early educational barriers mirrored the challenges I later faced in the public sector. For example, I once had to sign a large financial cheque quickly. While my colleagues were astonished at my willingness to take on such responsibility, I was confident in my understanding of the process and ensured all checks were in place. That evening, I explained to my curious colleagues that my in-depth understanding and meticulous attention to detail empowered me to make informed decisions swiftly.

Yet, my competence and willingness to help often brewed resentment rather than appreciation among my peers. This became evident during a year-end office crisis when all cashiers and their supervisors conveniently took leave, presumably to force me into seeking emergency assistance. Instead of panicking, I applied my knowledge of organisational processes and theories to efficiently resolve the issue, frustrating those who had hoped to see me fail.

Throughout my career, I have noticed that academic and professional settings often confuse mere advancement with genuine learning and understanding. The prevailing systems encourage manoeuvring for personal gain over genuine expertise and ethical behaviour, discouraging true intellectual growth and perpetuating mediocrity and envy.

Reflecting on these experiences, I realise that authentic learning involves understanding and applying knowledge to improve systems and make informed decisions, and not merely climbing the corporate or social ladder. As I navigated various bureaucratic and corporate environments, it became clear that real-world applications of academic theories were seldom implemented effectively, hindering progress in both public and private sectors.

These reflections are not merely criticisms but a call to recognise the importance of integrity, fairness, and genuine skills. By understanding these challenges and advocating for systemic changes, we can foster environments where true talent is recognised and rewarded, and where knowledge and fairness prevail over incompetence and corruption.

Expert Talk
Managing Your Finances and Business

Now, I cannot avoid who I am while interacting with you. I am a Chartered Accountant (CA), and the readers will eventually expect a pep-talk on managing their finances and exploring new business opportunities. We can say something about that such as, managing finances effectively is crucial for achieving financial stability and security.

Here is a summary of fundamental principles to help you manage your finances wisely:

- Track your expenses: Monitor where your money is going to understand your spending habits.
- Create a budget: Set realistic financial goals and allocate resources accordingly.
- Prioritise needs over wants: Distinguish between essential and discretionary expenses.
- Save and invest: Allocate a portion of your income towards short-term savings and long-term investments.
- Manage debt: Pay off high-interest loans and credit cards and avoid new debt.

- Build an emergency fund: Save three to six months' expenses for unexpected events.
- Diversify income: Consider multiple sources of revenue to reduce financial risk.
- Avoid lifestyle inflation: Avoid increasing spending as income grows; instead, direct excess funds towards savings and investments.
- Stay informed: Learn about personal finance and stay updated on economic trends.
- Avoid impulse purchases: Practise delayed gratification and thoughtful spending.
- Leverage tax-advantaged accounts: Utilise tax-deferred savings options such as:
  - Public Provident Fund (PPF)
  - Sukanya Samriddhi Yojana (SSY)
  - Employees Provident Fund (EPF)/Voluntary Provident Fund (VPF) schemes announced by the government from time to time
- Every year, buy some raw gold.
- Review and adjust: Regularly assess your financial progress and make adjustments as needed.

By following these principles, you will be well on your way to managing your finances effectively, achieving financial peace of mind, and securing a stable financial future.

Remember, managing finances is a long-term process requiring discipline, patience, and persistence. Start with small steps, and over time, you will develop healthy financial habits that will serve you well throughout your life.

However, I told you earlier that I am also writing this memoir to create a synergy between the spiritual and the material. You remember this, right? So, let me expand my thoughts in a wider context.

The country's profound spiritual heritage and pervasive belief systems act as a stabilising force in India's tumultuous socio-political landscape, where rapid development and deep-seated issues often threaten to push society towards anarchy. This deep-rooted spirituality, which transcends the vast array of religions practised across the nation, instils a sense of purpose and peace that often tempers the chaos of everyday life.

Indian spirituality, with its emphasis on *karma* (actions and their consequences), *dharma* (righteous duty), and *moksha* (liberation), encourages individuals to look beyond materialistic pursuits and find solace in higher purposes. This spiritual framework helps foster communal resilience. It is a collective understanding that despite the myriad challenges—from corruption to social inequities—a larger cosmic order balances the scales of justice and morality over time.

Moreover, the diverse belief systems in India cultivate a philosophy of acceptance. This acceptance is not about passive resignation but rather a profound acknowledgement of life's imperfections. It teaches that life's trials are obstacles and opportunities for growth and spiritual advancement. This perspective nurtures hope among the populace, a hope that someday, through collective and individual betterment, things will improve.

India's spirituality and belief systems thus serve as crucial pillars that uphold social order amidst potential chaos. They provide a buffer against anarchy and a foundational strength that encourages society to strive for harmony and progress. These values prompt individuals to think beyond personal gain and consider the community's well-being, fostering a spirit of cooperation and mutual respect essential for the nation's stability.

In essence, India's spirituality and entrenched belief systems are not mere relics of tradition but living, breathing forces that mould the character of its people and the nation's destiny. They keep the fabric of Indian society woven tightly, even when the pressures of modernity and conflict stretch it. By embracing and nurturing these spiritual and cultural underpinnings, India can continue to navigate its complex path toward development and social justice, anchored by its people's enduring hope and resilience.

As I approached my late forties, a newfound interest in business acumen took hold of me, spurred by the evolving dynamics in our corporate spheres and public sector enterprises. With twenty-eight years of service split between private and public sectors, it became increasingly clear that the fundamental understanding of creating and sustaining businesses—*vyapar ki samajh*—was conspicuously absent.

Technological advancements have revolutionised data science, yet the expected improvements in cost optimisation and process enhancement have devolved into indiscriminate cost-cutting measures nationwide. This misdirected approach has been exacerbated by a tender system prioritising cost over quality, leading to substandard products and services, often reliant on imports rather than fostering domestic production.

Business approaches globally: A comparative insight
Globally, the approaches to business vary significantly:
- **Business creation in the West:** In western Europe and the USA, the focus remains on innovative business creation,

driving growth through pioneering new markets and technological advancements.
- **Efficiency in Japan:** Japan has mastered refining business processes, emphasising energy efficiency and cost-effectiveness, which has been central to its industrial success.
- **Mass production in China:** Initially, China leveraged its vast land and labour resources to offer low-cost production facilities to businesses, prioritising volume over quality. However, recent developments indicate a shift towards quality improvement, learning from nations like South Korea and Thailand, which blend quality with competitive pricing.

In contrast, India's pursuit of economic gain at every level has led to declining standards, overshadowing the genuine passion for craftsmanship and quality that once characterised our artisans and businesses. The plight of these skilled workers underscores a national trend of devaluation in the name of progress.

From village fields to metropolitan bustle, I have observed a fundamental misunderstanding of money's role. It is often seen not as the medium of exchange it is intended to be but as an end goal, fostering greed, envy, and social decay. This misperception has degraded consumption standards, which are more about cultural richness than financial wealth.

Surprisingly, those who possess less often display a higher standard of living and enjoyment in their modest consumption compared to billionaires, who might own world-class brands, but lack sophistication in their lifestyle and consumption habits.

Historically, meals across Indian homes, both in rural and urban settings, were complemented by traditional beverages like whey, *kanji, jaljeera,* and *lassi.* These provided not only nutritional benefits but also a cultural richness to the dining experience. Their gradual disappearance from our dining tables, especially in a climate as demanding as India's, is both puzzling and indicative of a broader shift from traditional dietary habits towards a more homogenised global diet, losing touch with regional nutritional wisdom.

Misuse of public resources

An unfortunate reality in contemporary India is the elite's widespread entitlement attitude and influence in misappropriating public assets for personal gain. This is evident in upscale neighbourhoods where residents unlawfully extend their private spaces onto public roads or claim public land for personal use, reflecting a deeper social issue of resource entitlement and corruption. This behaviour undermines communal integrity and sets a detrimental precedent for civic responsibility and public stewardship.

Reflecting on these issues, it becomes clear that enhancing our understanding of business, the ethical use of resources, and maintaining cultural integrity are crucial for fostering a more equitable and prosperous society. This requires reevaluating our educational and policy-making frameworks to cultivate a generation that values ethical success over mere financial gain.

The misuse of the Indian Trust Act 1881, the Society Act 1860, and Section 8 of the Companies Act stands as a critical contributor to the entrenchment of poverty and the suppression of underprivileged classes in India.

These acts, designed to facilitate the operations of non-profit entities and ensure transparency and accountability in corporate governance, have often been exploited to siphon off funds meant for public welfare, perpetuating a cycle of corruption and economic disparity.

The Indian banking system, while comprehensive, suffers from significant flaws that detrimentally affect the nation's economy:

- **Non-Performing Assets (NPAs):** Taxpayers' money is frequently used to cover the losses from NPAs, indirectly funding banks' profits. This misuse of public funds contributes to a financial burden on the common citizen without any corresponding benefits.
- **Inefficient support for Small and Medium Enterprises (SMEs):** SMEs need more support from banking institutions to grow. Often, banks need to provide complete transparency or guidance through the loan process, leading to SMEs being saddled with unfavourable loan terms and excessive bureaucratic requirements.
- **Public sector banks:** Public sector banks typically accumulate substantial deposits from ordinary citizens. Then these banks often extend various loans to businesses and individuals. However, the process is marred by inefficiencies:
  - **Loan disbursement practices:** Bank officials might rush borrowers through the signing process without adequately explaining the terms, leading to a lack of clarity and potential financial distress for the borrower.
  - **Recovery practices:** To recoup loans, banks might resort to aggressive tactics like employing recovery agents or seizing collateral, which often does not align with the initially agreed-upon terms.
  - **Misallocation of loans:** There is an observed pattern where loans are preferentially extended to wealthy clients due to political or corporate pressures, neglecting the actual needy and viable businesses that could benefit the most from financial support.

The involvement of government bodies in real estate under the guise of development authorities has significantly inflated the cost of land, adversely affecting the manufacturing sector. This has led to:

- **Increased manufacturing costs:** As land costs soar, manufacturers have less capital to invest in quality machinery and skilled labour, reducing the sector's competitiveness and profitability.
- **Distortion of rural economies:** Development authorities often compensate villagers generously for land acquisitions, leading to sudden wealth among rural populations without corresponding economic activities or productivity. This newfound wealth can lead to social imbalance, with former farmers becoming rent-seeking landlords, further distancing them from productive economic contributions.

The transformation of rural areas into urban real estate projects without a corresponding improvement in urban infrastructure or living standards creates a disjointed urban landscape. Now wealthier, but lacking sustainable income sources, villagers often engage in political manoeuvring to maintain their newfound status, exacerbating social stratification and leading to governance challenges.

The overarching impact of these systemic issues perpetuates inequality and inefficiency, hampering India's potential for inclusive growth. Reforming the legal and regulatory frameworks governing trusts, societies, and corporate behaviour, as well as restructuring the banking sector's lending and recovery approach, is essential for fostering a more equitable economic environment. Addressing these issues will require a concerted effort from all government and civil

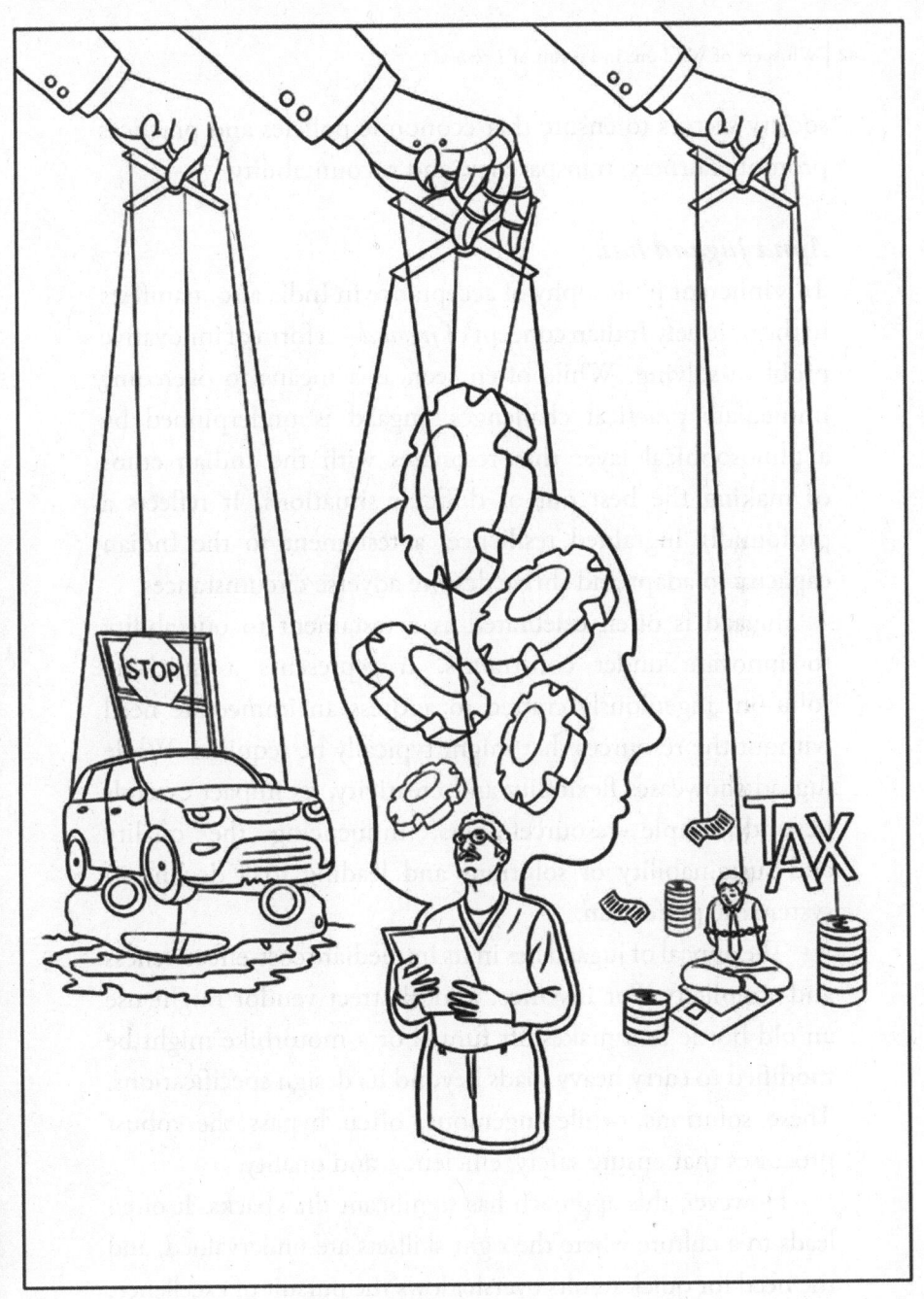

Life feels like a puppet show and you wonder who is pulling the tax strings

society sectors to ensure that economic policies and practices promote fairness, transparency, and accountability.

Apna jugaad hai!

This inherent philosophy of acceptance in India also manifests in the uniquely Indian concept of *jugaad*—a form of innovative problem-solving. While often seen as a means to overcome immediate practical challenges, jugaad is underpinned by a philosophical layer that resonates with the Indian ethos of making the best out of difficult situations. It reflects a profoundly ingrained resilience, a testament to the Indian capacity to adapt and thrive despite adverse circumstances.

Jugaad is often celebrated as a testament to our ability to innovate under constraints. It represents a quick-fix solution, ingeniously crafted to address an immediate need without the resources that might typically be required. While jugaad showcases flexibility and creativity, its impact extends beyond simple resourcefulness, influencing the quality and sustainability of solutions and leading to a decline in systematic perfection.

The appeal of jugaad lies in its immediate cost-effectiveness and simplicity. For instance, a local street vendor might use an old bottle as a makeshift funnel or a motorbike might be modified to carry heavy loads beyond its design specifications. These solutions, while ingenious, often bypass the robust processes that ensure safety, efficiency, and quality.

However, this approach has significant drawbacks. It often leads to a culture where the right skillsets are undervalued, and the need for quick results overshadows the pursuit of excellence. Over time, this can erode the foundation of professional standards and hinder business growth and learning advancement.

When your ride is more jugaad than speed

In socio-political and corporate realms, the jugaad mentality extends to interpersonal dynamics, where flattery becomes a tool for advancement. In these environments, individuals may engage in excessive praise or sycophancy to gain favour with their superiors. This behaviour stifles genuine talent and skill and promotes a culture where superficiality trumps substance.

Traditionally, intelligence is misinterpreted as the ability to succeed in academia or secure high-ranking positions. However, accurate intelligence encompasses the ability to foresee the long-term consequences of actions and decisions. An intelligent individual evaluates the broader implications of their choices, balancing short-term gains against long-term impacts.

A case study: Decision-making in a hotel

Consider the scenario in a hotel, where the general manager (GM) faces a decision about towel supplies. The supplier, attempting jugaad by offering more oversized towels at the price of medium ones due to a stock issue, presents what seems like a beneficial offer. The sourcing manager sees this as a gain, but the GM, thinking ahead, declines the offer.

While seemingly counterintuitive, the GM's decision is based on a deep understanding of the hotel's operational needs. He recognised that more oversized towels would require more space in service trolleys, leading to more trips and higher labour and laundry costs. This decision might appear as a loss in the short term, but it ultimately safeguards the hotel's operational efficiency and customer satisfaction.

While often lauded for its immediate benefits, the jugaad mindset can lead to compromised standards and efficient practices if balanced with a vision for long-term excellence. In business and governance, fostering a culture that values thoroughness and foresight over temporary fixes is essential for sustainable growth and innovation. This approach ensures that while creativity is encouraged, it does not come at the expense of quality and efficiency.

India's spirituality and belief systems thus serve as crucial pillars that uphold social order amidst potential chaos. They provide a buffer against anarchy and a foundational strength that encourages society to strive for harmony and progress. These values prompt individuals to think beyond personal gain and consider the community's well-being, fostering a spirit of cooperation and mutual respect essential for the nation's stability.

In essence, India's spirituality and entrenched belief systems are not mere relics of tradition but living, breathing forces that mould the character of its people and the nation's destiny. They keep the fabric of Indian society woven tightly, even when the pressures of modernity and conflict stretch it. By embracing and nurturing these spiritual and cultural underpinnings, India can continue to navigate its complex path toward development and social justice, anchored by its people's enduring hope and resilience.

However, a sad development is the falling of gullible women into the laps of charlatans presenting themselves as spiritual gurus. Women are frequently the main followers of spiritual leaders, often dubbed 'godmen' or 'godwomen.'

This widespread pattern can largely be traced to the profound psychological and social forces that shape the lives of many Hindu women, who find themselves trapped in a tightly bound, patriarchal web within their marital environment.

Across various social strata, the role of a woman is often distressingly compared to that of a domestic servant, with no viable alternative but to endure these oppressive structures. Relegated to the lowest tiers of family hierarchy, these women are subjected to persistent insults and a demeaning social order that erodes their dignity and self-worth.

In this context, the appeal of spiritual assemblies led by charismatic figures—revered *Babas* or deceitful charlatans—emerges as a beacon of refuge. These gatherings offer a unique space where women's voices and emotions are permitted and actively encouraged. Within the safe confines of these assemblies, women can express themselves openly, free from social judgment or censure. Activities such as dancing in a trance, which could attract negative attention or accusations of inappropriate behaviour outside these gatherings, are embraced and celebrated within such gatherings.

The role of the Baba in these settings is complex and multifaceted. To these women, he represents a singular male figure who validates their beauty and worth, listens to their difficulties with the empathy of a confidant, and welcomes them with warmth and understanding rather than disdain.

This contrasts sharply with the transactional and often conditional love they encounter daily. The Baba offers what seems to be an unconditional support system and guides them towards a path of spiritual emancipation, promising liberation from worldly attachments and social shackles that bind them.

Yet, this seemingly benevolent scenario also harbours the potential for exploitation, as these spiritual leaders might capitalise on the vulnerabilities of women confined by oppressive circumstances.

The influence of these Babas is not restricted to any single region. Still, it is a global phenomenon, tapping into the universal experiences of oppression and the human quest for meaning and acceptance. This dynamic often provides only an illusion of solace to its followers, particularly women, who might see these spiritual paths as their only escape from the harsh realities of their daily lives.

In this way, what is often perceived as a sanctuary can also be a place of subtle manipulation, highlighting the need for a more profound social change that genuinely empowers women and frees them from the underlying structures of domination and control.

These women devotees are blissfully ignorant of the fact that the majority of these so-called godly Babas have abandoned their families due to being tormented by their wives.

Rethinking my profession for you

There's a common misconception that chartered accountants are required solely for compliance services. However, this narrow perception is being challenged with the advent of artificial intelligence (AI). AI's role in transforming the field is significant, but it asks, 'Where will we bring the wisdom to operate such sophisticated technology effectively?'

Excessive motivation and recognition can paradoxically undermine the spirit of work excellence. A culture focused on accolades fosters a dependency on external validation rather than intrinsic motivation. This is evident in professional settings where individuals in leadership roles continuously seek recognition, diverting attention from the core objectives of their roles. This was particularly noticeable at a senior citizen conference, where the endless honours and awards ceremony overshadowed the true purpose.

In some professional circles, such as the legal field, I have observed that court proceedings are halted if an advocate or their relative passes away. While respectful, this practice can disrupt the judicial process, reflecting a broader issue of work culture overly reliant on traditional customs that may not always serve the best interests of justice or efficiency.

The adage, 'for growing up, change your friends and gossip circle,' might seem harsh at first glance, but it holds a more profound truth about personal and professional growth. To truly evolve and support those around you—friends, family, colleagues, and mentors—one must continuously develop social, educational, and macro-managerial skills, where economic prosperity is a natural consequence of these primary goals.

We absorb knowledge from educational institutions and books, which equip us with the theoretical tools needed for success. However, practical skills, such as courage, decisiveness, and the ability to act or 'pull the trigger,' are honed through real-world experiences in both work and leisure. The world is ever-changing, and to keep pace, one must adapt by constantly expanding their horizons.

Maintaining the same social circle without introspection can lead to stagnation. It is crucial to associate with people who avoid jealousy and aspire to grow alongside you. In my earlier years, I attempted to bring along peers who matched my pace, only to realise that they, too, sought advancement from others, sometimes at my expense.

Over time, it became clear that old acquaintances—often merely contacts rather than true friends—could harbour envy. Their concealed resentments could manifest as sabotage when opportunities arose. People generally seek relationships that offer them some form of benefit, whether immediate or anticipated, and they often gravitate towards those who can enhance their status or provide resources.

Every five years, consider elevating your social circle to include individuals who are a level above your current station. Annually, it is beneficial to let go of the least dynamic 20 per cent of your acquaintances to refresh your circle and stimulate continuous personal development. This does not mean abandoning old friends for materialistic reasons but rather prioritising relationships that are mutually enriching and aligned with your growth trajectory.

Imagine you have a network of five friends with varying levels of influence and resources:
- Rs 100 million in total assets
- Rs 150 million in total assets
- Rs 150 million in total assets
- Rs 200 million in total assets
- Rs 300 million in total assets

This sums up to a 'friendship wealth' of 900 million. After six years, instead of severing ties with friends worth 100 million, consider reallocating them within your broader network and seek to add a new contact worth 400 million. This strategy boosts your cumulative 'friendship wealth' to 1,300 million. In subsequent years, replace one of your 150 million friends with someone with a potential of 500 million, increasing your network's value to 1,650 million.

Here, 'friendship wealth' does not merely signify monetary value. It encompasses a formula where monetary value is just one component:
- Money (1x)
- Position (2x)

- Power (2x)
- Intelligence (3x)
- Loyalty (4x)
- Honesty (2x)
- Vision (6x)

Together, these attributes contribute to a comprehensive score that evaluates the true worth of your connections, ensuring they bring a balanced contribution of value, wisdom, and mutual support to your life.

This approach to networking encourages not just personal gain but a symbiotic growth where each connection is purposeful and enriching, steering clear of superficial interactions based solely on convenience or immediate benefit.

Zindagi ke saath, zindagi ke baad

Let us also talk about insurance. I know you have been waiting eagerly for this topic. The insurance premium combines savings along with the premium, so clubbing them together masks the actual product. Further, the insurance premium is based on an old mortality table, modified with so many loadings that its cost increases. The saving part is also not invested in the interest of policyholders; instead, it is invested in government agendas, leading to benefits for those who execute government projects.

Further, its high-cost ratio indicates inefficiency is loaded on the policyholder's pockets by charging more premiums and giving fewer bonuses. Further, its unit-linked policies are also subject to many flaws. People have lost their money in 'money plus' policies The insurance sales force agents and development officers have captivated the market to their advantage, hijacking the agenda and mission of this giant public organisation. The private sector has also gained the privilege of a giant public insurance company's footprints to the disadvantage of customers.

By the way, LIC stands for Life Insurance Corporation and not 'Life Investment Corporation.'

- I met a family who used to buy LIC policies and make fixed deposits (FDs) of Rs 1 lakh on each birthday of their children, and it has been 10 years since they have been doing so. Returns on these investments are a distant dream due to inflation. LIC ate up all their returns. The biggest scam that our parents' generation fell for was LIC. It locked in their money with little or even negative returns for decades. This might also be why the Indian middle class has never been able to create wealth.
- My family's total LIC premium is Rs 5.5 lakh plus per annum, locking up such big amounts for approximately 15 years more to come. This is the biggest scam, I tell my parents. Now we have started investing in mutual funds (MFs) starting three years ago.
- The purpose of an LIC policy is not for investment but for risk cover. Agents often push policies as investment options, which is incorrect. Investment and risk cover are different instruments. People are now taking LIC as insurance, not as an investment, and are looking for opportunities in different investment options.
- In a bullish market, every investor thinks that the stock market is a better investment. I cannot wait for the market to go sideways for five to seven years to slaughter investors like these. It is bound to happen. Nothing goes up forever. So, people should stop thinking that they are more

intelligent than the previous generation.
- A more giant scam is done by 'finfluencers' pitching futures and options (F&O) by showing fake screenshots. There is a burgeoning narrative among the youth, often influenced by finfluencers, that traditional investment avenues like LIC and FDs are outdated. Yet, in volatile markets, these traditional investments' conservative, albeit lower, returns might offer a safety net that pure market-linked investments do not. Previous generations had little or no information, so they fell for LIC. But at least they got some of their money back. However, despite all the information available online, the younger generation is losing money in F&O. F&O has destroyed the lives of many young investors who are falsely influenced by manufactured screenshots of high returns. In reality, most middle-class people are losing their money and capital in F&O.
- The old generation obtained more properties and lived stress-free lives, giving time to relationships. Wealth is made through multiple businesses, not by investment of money alone. This might work for 10 out of 11 people, but not for everyone.
- No one should buy unit-linked insurance policies (ULIPs) or endowment policies. The ULIP is an enormous fraud, especially for small business owners. One must invest for three to five years for a specific amount, and if by chance, one is unable to complete the tenure, the entire money is lost. There is no premature withdrawal for the policy as there is a cap of three or five years. Or there is a lock-in period. Our parents were so scared to lose their money and LIC milked their fears. After retirement, my father invested lakhs of rupees for 10 years in LIC ULIP schemes and Bajaj

Finance and received a meagre combined pension of Rs 18,000 per month.
- One cannot equate equity, systematic investment plans (SIPs) or MFs. We cannot compare insurance to equities. It is like comparing tomatoes to mangoes. Invest in MFs for investment purposes and opt for LIC for family protection. LIC and equities are both necessary. The stock market is gambling.
- The surrender value of a life insurance policy is also pretty bad. This makes people continue with the life insurance policy, which is obviously more damaging.

However, only a fool would think that LIC is a scam. LIC of India is such a big brand that many call all life insurance policies 'LIC.' This shows the trust and recognition that LIC has built over the years.

Most of the plans sold by LIC were endowment and money back plans, offering 6-7 per cent returns and risk coverage. These plans were never promoted as pure investments, and the premiums for these were mainly below Rs15,000 per year. LIC did offer ULIP, but people were not ready for market-based products then, leading many to surrender their policies out of fear of loss. It is also true that mutual funds have grown recently, but there are still very few people who have been doing regular SIP for fifteen to twenty years.

The LIC pension plan was the best in 2002. A friend bought a policy for Rs 2 lakh for 18 years. He paid Rs 11,000 per year. He is getting Rs. 50,000 a year. Had he invested Rs 4 lakh, he would have gotten Rs 1 lakh per year, a decent pension. Some safe returns, though low, are always better than unsecured or unsafe ones.

LIC is perhaps the most significant reason why insurance was not sold for the purpose it was meant for. It is because of the useless LIC plans sold for decades that the mindset of Indian customers towards pure life protection policies, like term plan life insurance policies, has been so dismal, as they do not get any money back on completion of the term.

The government exploited citizens in the name of providing financial security. LIC and LIC agents are the two actual beneficiaries of LIC policies. In fact, LIC was actually a guaranteed employment programme for agents. It is alleged that LIC was guaranteed both before and after death.

The biggest financial cobwebs in India are:
- Fast food culture
- Insurance
- Free porn

Two decades ago, people had limited avenues for investment. Therefore, FDs and LIC were the natural choices because of the TINA (There Is No Alternative) factor.

With the introduction of online banking and the digitisation of the share market, things are more accessible now. The irony is that the previous generation was saving something more than this generation.

Mindset: Even while buying a health insurance policy, people are tempted to ask if they will get back their premium. Indians think insurance *akele leke kya hoga. Kucch saath milna chahiye na?* Translation: it is not enough to be insured; one must receive something additional. Like *dhaniya* with *sabji* at the *sabjiwala*. Translation: Like one receives a complimentary bunch of fresh coriander leaves when one buys vegetables.

Because of the policy: 0.7 per cent;

WHY PEOPLE BOUGHT LIC POLICIES IN INDIA

To get your LIC agent uncle/friend/colleague off your back: 99.3%

The Life Insurance Corporation of India has long been a staple in Indian households, revered not just as a life insurance provider but as a critical investment vehicle. However, its premium structure reveals a complex blend of savings and insurance components, which can sometimes obscure the true cost and benefits of the policies.

LIC's premium structure combines insurance with a savings plan, making it difficult for policyholders to discern the insurance cost from the savings component. The premiums are often based on outdated mortality tables, with numerous loadings increasing costs. Moreover, the 'savings' portion of the premium is frequently invested in government projects, which may not always align with the best interests of the policyholders, potentially skewing the benefits toward governmental agendas rather than maximising returns for the policyholders.

LIC's operational model is marked by a high-cost ratio, suggesting inefficiencies that are passed down to policyholders through higher premiums and lower bonuses. ULIPs, which are meant to provide market-linked returns, have also been criticised for their high charges and poor performance, particularly noted during the downturn of policies like 'money plus.'

The dominance of LIC in the Indian market has allowed it to shape consumer perceptions and expectations around life insurance. Many families, like the one that invested in policies and FDs for their children, find themselves locked into long-term commitments that yield returns below inflation rates, effectively eroding their savings.

With the advent of mutual funds and more transparent financial products, the Indian populace is gradually shifting from viewing insurance solely as an investment to recognising it as risk coverage with separate investment avenues for wealth creation. However, this transition is not without its challenges.

As financial literacy improves, there is a growing awareness of the need for a diversified portfolio rather than reliance on a single investment mode. The understanding that insurance should not be conflated with investment is gaining ground, advocating for a clear distinction between risk coverage (insurance) and wealth generation (investment).

From 1 October 2024, as per the revised policy, a policyholder will get a higher refund if he exits his life insurance policy during the initial years. This is expected to provide greater flexibility and liquidity for life insurance customers who want to switch policies. Previously, surrendering a life insurance policy within the first year meant losing your entire premium.

This could be a significant financial setback, especially if you were mis-sold the policy or faced unforeseen circumstances.

However, things have changed with the introduction of the new Special Surrender Value (SSV) regulations by the Insurance Regulatory and Development Authority of India (IRDAI).

According to the revised norms by the insurance regulator IRDAI, life insurers must pay an enhanced SSV after the completion of the first year of the policy, provided the customer has paid one full year's premium. So far, companies have not paid such an amount to customers who surrender their policies in the first year.

A surrender value in insurance is the amount paid by insurers to a policyholder if he or she terminates the policy before its maturity date. If the policyholder surrenders during the policy's tenure, the earnings and savings portion will be paid to him or her.

Additionally, the norms stated that the discount rate for

discounting the paid-up value to calculate SSV will be allowed to be up to 50 basis points (bps) higher than the 10-year Government Security (G-Sec) yield.

Unlike earlier, when policyholders lost the entire premium paid if they exited the policy after year one, now they will get back a part of their premium.

Insurers' margins in the non-participating, guaranteed-return category of endowment plans will be the most affected.

There will be no change in the surrender value of unit-linked insurance policies and pure protection term covers.

Key changes

- **Enhanced SSV:** Under the new rules, policyholders who surrender their policies after the first policy year will receive a higher SSV than before.
- **Calculation formula:** The SSV must be at least equal to the present value of the paid-up sum assured, future benefits, and accrued/vested benefits, minus any survival benefits already paid.
- **Discount rate adjustment:** The discount rate used to calculate SSV has been increased by up to 50 basis points, resulting in higher payouts.

A policyholder who purchases a non-par endowment policy with an annual premium of Rs 1.2 lakh, a five-year premium paying term, and a tenure of 10 years will now receive Rs 1.06 lakh if they surrender after paying the first premium. Under the previous rules, the policyholder would have received nothing.

How it works

IRDAI specifies that the SSV calculation considers factors like the paid-up sum assured, future benefits, accrued bonuses, and survival benefits (if any), minus any already paid survival benefits. The interest rate used for this calculation cannot exceed the current yield on 10-year G-Secs plus an additional 50 bps.

The benefits for policyholders include the following:
- The revised rules offer greater flexibility to policyholders who may face financial difficulties.
- Policyholders forced to surrender their policies will experience a less severe financial loss.
- The new regulations aim to protect policyholders from unfair practices and give them more favourable terms.

The impact on life insurance companies includes the following:
- **Product revisions:** Life insurance companies had to revise their existing products to comply with the new regulations.
- **Deadline extension:** While companies sought a three-month extension, IRDAI maintained the original deadline.
- **Commission adjustments:** The new norms may impact commission structures for distributors.
- **Internal Rate of Return (IRR):** Changes in interest rates and surrender value calculations may affect customers' IRR.

Sovereign Guarantee

A sovereign guarantee is a guarantee provided by a government to secure debt or other financial obligations of a borrower, typically a public sector entity, state-owned enterprise, or private company undertaking a large infrastructure project.

This guarantee assures lenders that the government will cover any defaults or non-payment by the borrower.

Key features of sovereign guarantees include:
- **Government backing:** The guarantee is issued by a government agency or ministry.
- **Debt security:** It covers debt obligations, such as loans or bonds.
- **Payment assurance:** The government guarantees payment to lenders if the borrower defaults.
- **Credit enhancement:** Sovereign guarantees improve the creditworthiness of the borrower.
- **Risk mitigation:** Lenders face reduced credit risk due to government backing.

Sovereign guarantees are often used for:
- Infrastructure projects such as, transportation and energy
- Large-scale industrial projects
- Export financing
- Development projects in emerging economies

The benefits include:
- Increased investor confidence
- Lower borrowing costs
- Improved access to international markets

However, sovereign guarantees can also have drawbacks, such as:
- Contingent liabilities for the government
- Moral hazard as borrowers may take on excessive risk
- Potential impact on government credit ratings

The Indian government has reportedly extended various sovereign guarantees and support to the businesses of Adani and Ambani, among others, in the form of:

- **Letters of comfort:** Guarantees for specific projects or loans are provided to lenders.
- **Sovereign guarantees:** Explicit guarantees for loans or bonds issued by these companies.
- **Counter guarantees:** Guarantees provided to banks or financial institutions for loans extended to these companies.
- **Government undertakings:** Assurances for specific projects or investments are provided to lenders or investors. Some specific examples include:
  - **Adani Enterprises:** Received sovereign guarantees for loans related to infrastructure projects, such as power transmission and road construction.
  - **Adani Green Energy:** Received letters of comfort for loans related to renewable energy projects.
  - **Reliance Industries (Ambani):** Received sovereign guarantees for the Jamnagar refinery expansion project loans. They also got government undertakings for investments in the KG-D6 gas field.
  - **Reliance Jio Infocom:** Received sovereign guarantees for loans related to telecom infrastructure expansion. These guarantees are typically provided for specific projects or investments, and the details may not be publicly disclosed. The Indian government extends such support to various industries and companies, not just to Adani and Ambani, to promote economic growth and development.

LIC too, has a sovereign guarantee, which provides an added layer of security for its policyholders.

The government guarantees payment of LIC's insurance claims and also ensures LIC's solvency and financial stability.

Legal framework:
The sovereign guarantee is rooted in:
- The Life Insurance Corporation Act, 1956 (Section 37)
- The Insurance Act, 1938 (Section 124)

The key features are:
- **Government backing:** LIC is wholly owned by the Indian government.
- **Statutory guarantee:** The government guarantees the payment of insurance claims.
- **Solvency margin:** LIC maintains a solvency margin to ensure financial stability.
- **Regulatory oversight:** IRDAI monitors LIC.

The benefits to policyholders include:
- **Enhanced security:** Sovereign guarantee ensures payment of claims.
- **Trust and credibility:** Government backing instils confidence.
- **Financial stability:** LIC's solvency margin ensures long-term sustainability.

How sovereign guarantee works
LIC collects premiums from policyholders. Next, it invests the premiums in various assets. In case LIC faces financial difficulties, the government provides support and ensures the payment of insurance claims.

Some examples of the invocation of the sovereign guarantee are:

- 1972: The government guarantee helped LIC absorb losses from nationalisation.
- 1991: The government provided support during the economic liberalisation period.

Other insurance companies

Private insurance companies in India do not have an explicit sovereign guarantee. However, IRDAI regulates and monitors private insurers and private insurers maintain solvency margins. The Initial Public Offering (IPO) of LIC and recent changes to the LIC Act have implications for the sovereign guarantee.

IPO impact

LIC's IPO diluted government ownership from 100 per cent to around 95 per cent. It also changed the ownership structure—public shareholders now own approximately 5 per cent of LIC.

LIC Act amendments (2021)

- Section 37 amendment: Removes explicit sovereign guarantee for policyholders.
- Section 24 amendment: Allows LIC to invest up to 50 per cent of its assets in equity.

Impact on sovereign guarantee

The government still implicitly guarantees LIC's obligations. However, diluted ownership may impact the government's ability to provide explicit support, while policyholders and investors may perceive higher risk due to reduced government ownership.

Implications for policyholders

The implications for policyholders may involve a potential reduction in credit rating, as rating agencies may reassess LIC's creditworthiness.

This leads to an increased uncertainty, as policyholders may worry about government support.

Implications for investors

The implications for investors include a risk-return trade-off, where investors may demand higher returns due to a perceived increased risk.

This could lead to some market volatility as LIC ownership and guarantee changes may impact stock prices.

While LIC has played a pivotal role in providing financial security to generations, its role as an investment vehicle is being re-evaluated in today's economic landscape. The evolving financial markets and the increasing sophistication of Indian investors are prompting a re-examination of traditional investment strategies. Considering this, LIC's model, heavily reliant on traditional, conservative investment notions, may need to innovate and align more closely with contemporary financial realities to maintain its relevance and efficacy.

This expansion provides a broader view of the issues with LIC's premium structure while situating it within the larger context of changing investment trends in India.

In Pursuit of *Lakshmi*
Challenges and Conundrums

Lakshmi, the Hindu goddess of prosperity, beauty, and good fortune, embodies the spiritual aspects of abundance, inner light, and divine feminine energy. Her presence in Hindu mythology and worship offers a profound spiritual significance that transcends material wealth. Spiritually, Lakshmi represents the abundance of the universe, reminding us that life is full of endless possibilities and resources. She embodies the energy of manifestation, inspiring us to dream big and have faith in the universe's generosity. Her presence encourages us to cultivate a sense of gratitude and appreciation for the blessings in our lives.

Lakshmi is also associated with the light of knowledge, guiding us toward spiritual growth and enlightenment. Her radiance symbolises the illumination of our inner selves, dispelling ignorance, and darkness. As we invoke her presence, we are reminded to seek wisdom, intuition, and inner guidance.

As a symbol of divine feminine energy, Lakshmi embodies the qualities of receptivity, nurturing, and compassion. She reminds us of the importance of self-care, self-love, and self-worth. Her energy encourages us to embrace our femininity, creativity, and emotional depth.

In spiritual practices, Lakshmi is often invoked to bring balance and harmony into our lives. Her presence is believed to purify our energy, attracting positive vibrations and repelling negativity. Through her worship, we seek to cultivate a sense of inner peace, joy, and contentment.

Lakshmi's spiritual significance extends beyond the material realm, inviting us to explore the depths of our own inner richness. She reminds us that true prosperity lies in the abundance of love. However, when we encounter Lakshmi and pursue her, it leads us in different directions. Let me recount an anecdote.

One night, I was messaging a founder whose journey and company I deeply admire and respect. His response was heart-wrenching. He wrote, 'My life is such a whirlpool these days, and I can't express it.'

This entrepreneur, who has made substantial innovations and impacted India profoundly, feels overwhelmed and helpless. His words resonated with me, echoing my challenges with the feared 'angel tax' that has jeopardised our business. We faced 18 days in financial limbo, with frozen accounts and seized bank funds, battling a tax that nearly crippled us.

The journey of entrepreneurship in India is uniquely challenging. We operate in a realm where we are presumed guilty until proven innocent. If you ever feel alone, the isolation of an entrepreneur in India is incomparable.

Despite the turmoil, we must maintain a facade of

happiness, continually inspiring others while navigating our storms. Regardless of external pressures or market dynamics, we are expected to consistently deliver—to investors, clients, employees, and customers.

Entrepreneurs are seen as superhuman and expected to have solutions for every problem. We juggle relationships and build trust, all while masking our struggles. We are supposed to walk confidently, hiding any pain or disability from the world. The words 'no' and 'not possible' are not in our vocabulary. We cannot afford to show vulnerability or share our burdens openly. We shoulder everyone's problems and strive to resolve them.

Despite being coated in dust and sweat, we must appear joyful and fulfilled. We battle tirelessly, always ready to rise after a fall, and bleed only to be seen as warriors in the arena.

Yet, for all our resilience and valour, an entrepreneur's most constant companion is loneliness. True entrepreneurship demands that you embrace this solitude as part of the journey.

The prevailing challenges faced by Indian entrepreneurs today can be traced back to the legacy of the British colonial era. During this time, Indian business persons supported the freedom fighters by providing logistical and monetary assistance, a narrative often overshadowed by the political and bureaucratic frameworks established post-independence.

These frameworks have persisted due to political naivety and a need for more administrative savvy among the politicians who took over after independence. This situation has been further exacerbated by the entanglement of politics within bureaucratic constraints, allowing only a few to monopolise the nation's wealth, including natural resources and emerging business opportunities presented globally.

Karma and *Nirvana* are your two options but you are just here for an enlightenment upgrade

Profit in India is often perceived negatively, viewed as a form of loot or extortion rather than a reward for the risk and effort invested in building a business from the ground up. As an independent nation striving to develop, there is a critical need to shift this perception. We should aim to increase the proportion of earned income, such as profits and salaries while diminishing the relative ease of earning through rent and interest, which does not actively contribute to national development.

Over the past seventy-five years, there have been vital lessons that we have failed to grasp, lessons that are crucial for propelling India to the forefront of industrial production and business. These lessons are as follows:

- **Role of developed nations:** The primary function of developed countries is to foster business growth domestically by increasing their people's incomes, which boosts tax revenues.
- **Domestic business challenges:** In India, however, entrepreneurs face numerous obstacles. Despite these challenges, if an entrepreneur manages to thrive, contributing to Gross Domestic Product (GDP) growth and employment and investing heavily in employee training, they are further burdened by an educational system ill-suited for business needs. Rather than receiving support, they face taxation.
- **Lack of support:** It is disheartening to note the absence of significant political or governmental assistance for businesses. Instead of support, companies often face extortion from various quarters, including those posing as charity seekers.
- **Role of development authorities:** Perhaps the most

detrimental aspect has been the role of development authorities, which have set the nation back by a century. These authorities sell industrial land at exorbitant prices, with limited and unreliable utility supply, causing land in the market to appreciate much faster than the industries can grow. Entrepreneurs allocate up to 80 per cent of their capital to land acquisition and only 20 per cent to machinery, furniture, and working capital. This skewed investment leads to operational losses within five years, although profits can sometimes be recouped by selling the land at triple the purchase price.

This systemic inefficiency calls for a profound re-evaluation of how businesses are supported and nurtured in India. A paradigm shift is necessary from viewing business merely as a source of tax revenue to recognising it as a fundamental driver of national prosperity and development.

Another friend confided in me, 'I am an associate to one of the largest agribusiness startups not only in India but the world—same story. The lack of empathy from the government agencies controlling the business is killing, and no one except the founders know about it. It is a person's worst nightmare.'

A wag quipped, 'Don't be so heartless. If we don't tax these highly productive people, how can we feed Ashok and his wife with free food and rations?'

It is damning evidence of how business in India has floundered to the point of no return and to the cause of joblessness as well as the demise of democracy. It's a similar story with all Micro, Small, and Medium Enterprises (MSME) entrepreneurs in India; all of them are looking down the barrel of a gun with severe liquidity problems.

At the same time, corruption in India is a pervasive and deeply entrenched problem that affects various aspects of Indian society. According to Transparency International's 2023 Corruption Perception Index, India ranks ninety-three out of one hundred and eighty countries, indicating a high level of corruption.

However, corruption has never been an issue in this part of the world for centuries, which is why it will always grow with the continuous watering of *chaplusi* or sycophancy and with the regular manure of 'power worshipping,' killing all fairness and assertiveness kind of pests and insects while continuously improving the strength of hatred and jealousy. This beautiful fructuous tree, incorrectly called corruption, is protected with the strong metal of 'gang culture.'

Further, any hint of a move to harm corruption is quickly thwarted by the strong army of 'god protectors' and 'social contractors' 'with the cover fire of intellect-filled journalism.'

Any positive action is quickly fizzled out by the wonderful navy of the 'shouting brigade.' Such a strong defence mechanism is made best globally with the world's best technology and digital missiles.

With apologies to all defenders of this century-old heritage, I learned the web of defence mechanisms in childhood, which I understood later in depth with increasing age and exposure to 'rewinding memory.'

Some examples: 'First I was snubbed at the age of nine years by a very learned stalwart of my town for asking, if 'Maharaja Harish Chandra was *satyavadi* and suffered due to following the path of truth then what about other inhabitants of that era, were they not speaking the truth?' At the age of 17, I was hounded by gentlepersons with multiple degrees when I asked, 'If we were most intelligent and brave in the world then why were we invaded and ruled by demons starting from the Lodhis, Britishers and other *netas*?' In answer to which they called me names. However, I still hold that we may have got one of the most honest polities, but not the most talented one in the world.

Finally, a nasty nail was pierced into my consciousness to sharpen my understanding when I questioned my Economics professor in 1988. If we were an excellent economy called the 'golden bird' with the highest GDP, then why did 66 per cent of the population not have their own houses, and 22 per cent of the population lived in mud houses with a thatched roof? Only 12 per cent had a *pucca* house. That professor had predicted that I would never be successful if I questioned the country's intellect.

Later, I met a mighty politician who praised the pre-Moghul era as the best on earth in this part of the world. I nodded in support of his love for our motherland, where he focused on seeing the best of the king, lords, and their henchmen, with huge palaces made up of the world's best materials and great architectural beauty but surrounded by poor people with no pucca houses. Once again, my apologies to all.

We have the dubious distinction of possessing:
- **Red tape and corruption:** Excessive regulations, complex procedures, and corrupt practices hinder efficient decision-making and service delivery.
- **Inefficiency and slow decision-making:** Bureaucratic processes are often slow, leading to delays in project implementation, policy decisions, and public service delivery.
- **Lack of accountability:** Insufficient transparency and accountability mechanisms enable bureaucratic inertia and unresponsiveness.

- **Resistance to change:** Bureaucratic rigidity and aversion to reform, hinder adaptation to changing needs and circumstances.
- **Nepotism and favouritism:** Unmerited appointments, promotions, and transfers based on personal connections rather than merit.
- **Inadequate training and capacity building:** Bureaucrats often lack the necessary skills, knowledge, and expertise to perform their roles effectively.
- **Political interference:** Excessive political influence over bureaucratic decisions and actions undermines impartiality and effectiveness.
- **Hierarchical and siloed structure:** Communication and coordination challenges arise from a rigid hierarchical structure and isolated departments.
- **Lack of citizen engagement:** Insufficient public participation and consultation in decision-making processes.
- **Outdated rules and procedures:** Bureaucratic frameworks often fail to meet changing social needs and technological advancements. These issues contribute to a perception of Indian bureaucracy as slow, unresponsive, and ineffective, hindering the country's development and governance. However, efforts are being made to address these challenges through administrative reforms and initiatives aimed at improving efficiency, transparency, and accountability.

India's development trajectory differs from Australia's and Canada's due to various historical, economic, and social factors. Here are some key reasons:

- **Colonial legacy:** India was a British colony for nearly two centuries, which drained its resources and hindered industrialisation. Australia and Canada were also colonies but benefited from British investment and technology transfer.

- **Post-independence:** After gaining independence in 1947, India faced immense poverty, illiteracy, and infrastructure gaps. Australia and Canada, already developed, continued to grow steadily.
- **Economic policies:** India adopted socialist-oriented policies, leading to a large public sector and state control, whereas Australia and Canada embraced free market economies, encouraging private enterprise and foreign investment.
- **Population growth:** India's rapid population growth, from 350 million in 1947 to 1.4 billion today, has had a profound impact on its development trajectory. This growth has put significant pressure on resources, infrastructure, and services, a challenge not faced by Australia and Canada, which have relatively small populations.
- **Corruption and governance:** India's struggle with corruption and bureaucratic inefficiencies has significantly impeded effective governance and development. In contrast, Australia and Canada boast robust institutions and governance systems.
- **Investment in education and healthcare:** Australia and Canada invested heavily in education and healthcare, creating a skilled workforce and healthy population. India's progress in these areas has been slower.
- **Globalisation and trade:** Australia and Canada have benefitted from globalisation and are more open to international trade and investment. India has only recently begun to liberalise its economy.
- **Geography and natural resources:** Australia and Canada have vast natural resources, while India's geography is more

- **Historical conflicts and political instability:** India has faced numerous conflicts and political instability, diverting resources and attention from development. Australia and Canada have enjoyed relative peace and stability. These combined factors have contributed to the differing development paths of India, Australia, and Canada. However, India has made significant progress in recent years and continues to grow and develop rapidly.

I apologise to every human, flora, and fauna of this part of the world. My views are a little erratic and very difficult to hear. Education via books is only 10 per cent, and 30 per cent is in your socio-economic environment. The remaining 60 per cent lies in your quest for learning by connecting dots, with skill, and humility. A society can overhaul this in six generations if it is continually made to do so by people with different kinds of power to captivate your thinking.

Returning to the point of my unwanted, irrational rewinding quest, I feel that despite dynamic improvement in society, the Crown is not ready to lose its grip over the world.

The Crown is not an individual but an institution of best retained macro leaders capable of tweaking each micro. So, this institution has been much ahead of the world in designing the structure of social, religious, administrative, and political ribs that are kept alive by the flowing blood of the economic stream. This point litmus test is a family holding power for 1,200 years by keeping its clout together. This clout not only involves 250 odd family members but also the top percent of social, religious, and business leadership.

It has kept hold by its continuous cumulative synergy to

weave an economic and administrative net. This net is further strengthened by various knots like the UN and its extended arms, G-7, G-20, trade agreements and inter-country block of nations uncounted treaties, conventions, resolutions, and money, plus goods/services interwoven trails.

Chasing development

Migration to cities is due to the lack of basic civic amenities in villages, which are crucial for psychological and physiological needs. Village cohesiveness is missing due to a rising religious uproar. Keeping the rising sentiments of youngsters, particularly women, suppressed in the garb of our culture, ethos, and rituals, are now ineffective due to the upheaval caused by the rising use of technology and communication methods.

The reason for the lack of social cohesiveness has many hidden reasons. One is that the pricing of goods and services in different sectors is too erratic due to the vested interests of crony politics and civil servants who take advantage of political incompetence. Moreover, the hatred and jealousy created by political rivalry are accentuated by the so-called religious and caste leaders.

The greed for money is rising due to a power culture and reward system, not for work, but due to the name of a person. Villagers love to be litigants, even for petty issues. Why? This problem is more due to genetics and less due to a discriminatory budgetary allocation.

By and large, the population of this part of the world has been more quarrelsome due to their fear of big wars. Every human has a fighting instinct, and it is satiated at home due to a lack of courage to fight with bigger enemies. We as a

Rush hours get bumpy with mismatching resource allocations

nation have no history of winning a war except in 1971, that too under the leadership of a woman. Even Churchill decided to create a strong army before giving independence. His parliamentary speeches tell a lot about the skill of writing beautifully crafted speeches and the absence of warrior forces in some parts of the northern belt.

So far, urbanites are less litigant than villagers. Because the urban population earns more from wages than from rentals and interest, they fear the cost of court litigation in terms of time and money.

I was born in Moradabad and later moved to Delhi/Noida in 1984. I have not seen even a single day without petty squabbling, whether at the workplace or in the neighbourhood, shopping places, parking areas, at conferences, meetings, social gatherings, and festivals.

Whether in the city or in the village, we get pleasure in arguing, petty fighting, cursing other castes, religions, and families, rather than in relishing better quality and more variety of food and beverages. We discuss more people, things, and ideas that have rarely been seen by us in our lifetime. Something portrayed as an idea in India, was actually the political or economic agenda of the West and the USA. A recent example is environmental consciousness and going digital without braking, steering, or honking.

India is a large country that is overpopulated and is not sheltered by any nation, except Great Britain, which our people hate. The first Prime Minister, Mr Nehru, wanted to have a different foundation for growth other than being liked by Britain, and the most popular leader, Mr Gandhi, sustained a village economy, which was followed by entire Europe.

Staying away from war in such a situation leads to internal squabbling. The same can be observed in any family in a rural or urban area. Where families struggle with the outside world for their growth and success, they remain united, and when there is no struggle, they have petty issues even in a nucleus family.

Around the World and a few Provocations

The art of provocation is a potent tool to challenge social norms, spark critical thinking, and inspire change. It involves using creative expression to confront and disrupt the status quo, often through controversial or unconventional means. Artists, writers, and thinkers have long employed provocation to stimulate dialogue, expose hypocrisy, and push boundaries. Adequate provocation requires a deep understanding of the audience and the context in which the work is presented. It must be carefully crafted to balance shock value with substance, avoiding gratuitous offence or alienation. The goal is to prompt reflection, not simply to inflame or outrage.

One of the most significant benefits of provocation is its ability to challenge groupthink and conventional wisdom. Artists and writers can force audiences to re-examine their assumptions and consider new ideas by presenting alternative perspectives or uncomfortable truths. This can lead to a more informed and engaged citizenry better equipped to address complex social issues.

However, provocation can also be misused or misunderstood. Some may employ it as a cynical marketing ploy or attention-seeking tactic, prioritising shock value over substance. In such cases, the art of provocation devolves into mere sensationalism, undermining its potential for meaningful impact.

Ultimately, the art of provocation is a delicate balancing act, requiring both courage and nuance. When wielded thoughtfully, it can be a powerful catalyst for growth, innovation, and social change. As we navigate an increasingly complex and polarised world, the art of provocation offers a vital means of stimulating critical thinking, challenging entrenched power structures, and fostering a more inclusive and empathetic society.

Let me take this opportunity to provoke my readers with this chapter based on some of my observations. It goes without saying that the utility of this exercise is to provoke responses.

A darkly humorous adage reflects a cynical view of various professions, suggesting that many professionals in service industries benefit from the misfortunes of others. This perspective highlights an often-overlooked aspect of economic incentives in specific jobs, where professionals stand to gain when others need their services.

The joke states that many professionals thrive from misfortune.

Here is an expanded version with more detailed examples:
- **Lawyer:** Traditionally seen as one who benefits from disputes and legal troubles, lawyers are often joked about as ones who are hoping for conflict or legal issues because their expertise becomes essential and their services are in demand.
- **Doctor:** It is said that a doctor's business thrives due to the ailments of others. While doctors are committed to

healing, the nature of their profession inherently means they are needed more when people are unwell.
- **Police officer:** This role is essential to maintain law and order, yet a police officer's job security depends upon a steady flow of criminal activity.
- **Teacher:** While educators aim to enlighten their students, the joke on them would suggest that they benefit from students who need extra help or tutoring, highlighting the demand for their guidance.
- **Landlord:** Landlords make a living by renting out properties, hence, theoretically, they benefit from a market where buying a home is out of reach for many, ensuring a continuous pool of renters.
- **Dentist:** Like doctors, dentists help maintain dental health, but cavities and dental issues keep their schedules full and businesses profitable.
- **Mechanic:** A mechanic's expertise is most sought after when vehicles malfunction. Hence, it is joked that mechanics secretly hope for vehicle breakdowns to ensure a steady stream of work.

In contrast to these, the joke concludes with a thief, humorously noted to be the only one who wishes you prosperity and sound sleep. Why? Because the more prosperous you are, the more there is for the thief to steal, and a sound sleep ensures easy theft without interruption.

This joke starkly illustrates a paradox where certain professionals might seem to benefit from others' misfortunes while serving crucial social roles. It is a humorous reflection on the dual nature of many professions, where the intention to serve and the nature of their benefit from society's woes can coexist.

When you realise mid-heist that counting the loot by hand was a bad choice

Dominance of the British Crown

The influence of the British Crown in the modern world extends well beyond the direct governance of its former colonies. Although the British Empire formally ended in the mid-twentieth century, the monarchy continues to wield significant symbolic and practical influence across global affairs.

Here's a more detailed glance at the mechanisms through which the British Crown's legacy and the United Kingdom (UK) shape international dynamics.

The British monarch remains the ceremonial head of the Commonwealth, a group comprising of 56 member states, including many former colonies. This role helps promote a shared set of governmental and cultural values rooted in the British tradition.

London maintains its status as a leading global financial centre. The influence of British financial institutions and the regulatory frameworks they operate under can be felt worldwide, affecting international markets and economic policies.

The English language and British cultural products—from literature to television and educational systems—continue to profoundly impact the world. This cultural export facilitates a form of soft power that the UK wields internationally.

The UK's extensive diplomatic connections, fostered through both the royal family and its government, enable it to play a pivotal role in international affairs, advocating for global cooperation and stability.

As a symbol of continuity and tradition, the British monarchy enhances the UK's image globally, often being perceived as a stabilising element in international relations. The UK's historical and ongoing treaty relationships grant it preferential trade agreements and strategic military bases around the globe, enhancing its ability to project power and influence foreign policies.

The UK's active participation in major international bodies like the UN, NATO, the G-7, and the G-20 allows it to influence global policy, from security to economic development.

The UK has secured Bilateral Investment Treaties (BITs) with numerous countries, safeguarding British investments abroad and often giving British companies advantageous positions in foreign markets.

Historical and ongoing secret agreements, such as the UK-USA Security Agreement, underscore the depth of the UK's influence in international intelligence and security realms.

The UK has been instrumental in developing international law, and British legal principles and practices influence judicial systems worldwide. Through its significant economic capabilities and position in global finance, the UK can exert influence over global monetary policies and financial stability.

British intelligence agencies maintain global operations that protect UK interests and provide critical intelligence to allies, shaping international security strategies. Though diminished, the UK's control over several crown dependencies and overseas territories gives it strategic military and economic advantages in key world areas. The allure of the British culture, supported by its royal heritage and institutions like the British Broadcasting Corporation (BBC), continues to promote UK values and perspectives globally, enhancing its diplomatic relationships.

These elements together illustrate how the British Crown and the broader UK governance structure continue to exert a comprehensive and nuanced influence on world affairs, proving that their impact is historical and deeply ingrained in the current global framework.

Where are Smart Cities?

Now is the time for unequivocal candour, a moment to confront the profound shortcomings that plague our cities—a degree of incompetence, corruption, and ineptitude unprecedented in India's history. I am weary of hearing boasts about India's Smart Cities program when in reality, these so-called intelligent cities are too often administered by individuals whose actions suggest they care little for their constituents. These administrators view urban decay as a highbrow concern, irrelevant to their electoral success, oblivious to the lasting damage inflicted on India's reputation as an investment haven and tourist destination. The enduring tragedy is that these miscreants continue their malpractices unchecked and unchallenged by the public and the judiciary.

In our era, why should cities like Delhi and Gurugram or states like Goa collapse under the strain of a single heavy monsoon? Why must innocent lives be jeopardized by municipal negligence, or the elderly live in dread of their homes flooding? Our complacency as a populace, dazzled by short-term political freebies, diverts attention from assessing the true capabilities of our leaders, laying bare the deficiencies for all to see.

The decay of urban India is stark: bridges collapse, tunnels flood, roads cave-in, and citizens endure abject conditions despite dutifully paying their taxes, with little to no governmental response. Our parliamentarians seem more interested in curating social media presences amid these crises than in voicing concerns in parliament, where petty squabbles overshadow substantive governance. This is not just disappointing; it is downright disgraceful.

Consider Gurugram, a city housing some of India's

foremost corporations, hospitals, and luxurious residences. Residents navigate through waterlogged streets, sidestep garbage, and dodge open manholes. The state's Chief Minister appears disengaged from these governance failures—starkly contrasting the Bhartiya Janta Party's (BJP's) proclamations of ensuring good governance.

In Goa, the story is no better. Panjim, purportedly an intelligent city, resembles a dystopian landscape with its perpetually dug-up streets and unending construction. It leaves the public to suffer alone, as government officials remain insulated from the consequences. Similarly, Mumbai's local trains transform into veritable death traps with each monsoon, and the city comes to a standstill, as if this disruption is a natural consequence rather than a failure of infrastructure maintenance.

How much longer can we tolerate this? While our leaders boast internationally of India's prowess, the reality speaks of a nation failing to master the fundamentals. From airports with roofs susceptible to the wind, to hill stations crumbling under their weight, the narrative of failing infrastructure has become all too common.

The genuinely disheartening part is the lack of accountability. Offenders continue unscathed, and the populace, numbed by recurring crises, braces for the next disaster. I would argue for severe penalties for those responsible, yet even that seems a distant reality.

As an optimist, I travel across India hoping for signs of progress. Still, the evident decay leads me to an unhappy conclusion: not even divine intervention can correct our course. Even Lord Ram's fabled abode in Ayodhya has not been spared from leaks. It is time for profound reflection on our part as a nation—are we doomed to watch our cities crumble, or will we demand the governance we truly deserve?

Non-Resident Indians: Long-distance nationalism

For many Indians, the overarching goal often seems to be in escaping the multifaceted challenges of their homeland. This escape can manifest in two ways: physically relocating to another country or secluding oneself within the fortified sanctuaries of gated communities. Both avenues offer a retreat from the daily rigours and systemic issues that permeate life in India, from infrastructure woes to bureaucratic inefficiencies.

Once removed from the immediate problems, whether through emigration or by isolating themselves in well-manicured enclaves that bear little resemblance to the surrounding urban sprawl, Indians often adopt a rosier view of their motherland. The seemingly impossible frustrations from a safe distance now blur into a nostalgic haze. India is reimagined as a flawless homeland, unblemished by the genuine issues left behind.

This phenomenon is not unique to India; it is a typical human response to distance oneself from discomfort and complexity. However, it highlights a particular cultural contradiction: the homeland is simultaneously shunned for its faults and venerated once those faults are no longer a daily nuisance. This duality can inhibit constructive dialogue and meaningful action toward improvement, as the expatriate community may hold onto an idealised image of India that resists acknowledgement of its ongoing issues.

Furthermore, the mindset of escaping India reflects a more profound social disillusionment. For those who leave, India symbolises the never-fully realised potential. At the same time, for those who retreat into gated communities, it represents a paradise that must be cordoned off from the chaos of everyday life. In both cases, there is an underlying resignation—a belief that outside the gates or across the oceans lies a better quality of life, inaccessible within the broader Indian context.

The romanticisation of India by those who have left its shores often turns into advocacy for a homeland that no longer aligns with the lived realities of those who remain. This idealisation can perpetuate a cycle where the diaspora invests more in preserving the myth of what India could be rather than in addressing what it is.

To truly honour the nation, those who leave and those who stay in their gated refuges, both must engage with India's complexities. They should contribute their global experiences and resources towards tangible improvements and realistic solutions rather than secluding themselves from the challenges that need addressing. Only then can the cycle of disillusionment and idealisation be broken, replaced with a proactive engagement that cherishes India for what it is while striving earnestly for what it could become.

My personal experiences reflect this broader social issue. Growing up in a crime-prone area known for its *dadagiri* or thuggish behaviour, I witnessed how coercive tactics were used to extort 'donations' for various causes, with the funds seldom reaching their intended purposes.

In my first job in a medium-sized company, the work environment was rife with indiscipline and casual mistreatment from senior staff who enjoyed belittling newer employees. However, my employers taught me a valuable lesson about work ethic—that increasing one's hours of dedicated work can surpass even the most privileged or seemingly advantaged colleagues—helping me maintain my professional integrity and focus.

This early professional milieu was characterised by a lack of support for meritocracy and an overemphasis on connections and influence, a dynamic prevalent in both public and private sectors. It became evident that in many organisations, especially in public services, mediocrity was often institutionalised, stifling innovation and discouraging talented individuals who were motivated to make meaningful contributions.

Let me lobby for you

The 'lobby culture' I encountered has significantly held back our nation's progress, fostering an environment that might often override right. This pervasive issue affects everyday interactions, whether in driving, shopping, or social gatherings, where systemic inefficiencies and corrupt practices prevail, undermining the potential for genuine social advancement.

Reflecting on these experiences, I believe that for India to advance genuinely, we must cultivate a culture that prioritises integrity, merit, and civic responsibility. Only by addressing these fundamental issues can we hope to foster a more equitable, efficient, and prosperous society.

After completing my studies, I moved to Delhi, became a chartered accountant, and joined the public sector. Despite the prevalence of uncivil behaviour and numerous challenges, my time in Delhi was a period of significant personal and professional growth. I learned much about civic responsibility amidst the city's chaos—where a lack of basic civic sense is evident in everyday scenarios like traffic management, public services, and general public behaviour. While often difficult, this environment provided a rich backdrop against which I could develop a robust understanding of social dynamics.

Starting my journey in a metropolitan city in 1984, I faced numerous challenges, mainly due to a lack of financial resources. Many people cheated me ruthlessly during this time. Auto rickshaw drivers never missed an opportunity to overcharge me; once, I was charged an exorbitant Rs 50 for a short ride from Scindia House to the fire station in Connaught Place.

During my training, I joined a medium-sized company where the atmosphere was marked by indiscipline and gossip. Seniors took pride in mocking me and squandering money, creating a hostile environment. However, my employers were kind-hearted and imparted a valuable lesson: if they could complete a task in four hours and I took eight, I should increase my working hours to surpass them. Since then, I have become dedicated to my work, not out of greed for money but to maintain my dignity. This work ethic gave me the strength and confidence to excel, regardless of whether I was in a government or corporate setting. I always strived to do my best in the organisation's best interest.

The pervasive lobby culture in public and private sectors has significantly hindered our nation's progress. Many people prioritise power over justice in the workplace, personal, and social life. Our bureaucracy is designed to spoil rather than to build a career.

I quickly realised mediocrity was the norm in my public sector experience. Despite this realisation, I remained in the public sector for 16 years for personal reasons, though I did not enjoy a single day. Youngsters often join such organisations with great talent and ambition, but the strong culture of mediocrity diminishes their vision over time.

A lousy carpenter makes the worst furniture from the best timber, while a good carpenter can create masterpieces from flawed wood. Unfortunately, I never encountered such skilled 'carpenters' in my professional journey.

After leaving the public sector, I joined a private company that had partnered with a German firm. From the outset, I noticed that Standard Operating Procedures (SOPs) were systematically dismantled. Following the SOPs led to being sidelined and mocked. People tend to undermine sound systems, seeking comfort in mediocrity, which is evident in daily life—whether on the road, while shopping, or at social gatherings.

Discipline and Cleanliness

I recall my first visit to a foreign country, where I was astonished by their disciplined behaviour. There was no honking, no zigzag driving (which we often consider smart driving), and people formed orderly queues at shops, waiting patiently for their turn. The shopkeepers also adhered to this system, serving one customer at a time. However, this system is often broken by the wealthy, dominant classes, and so-called educated masses back home, who behave like bullies. This difference in behaviour is a daily experience.

When I first saw the cleanliness abroad, with efficient garbage collection and streets being washed for two hours every night, I thought our government did not care about cleanliness. However, I later realised that the flaw lies in people's upbringing, who often display rowdy behaviour with pride. *Inki bahut baat hai* (they have a lot of influence) is a common punch line that signifies power.

Further, not sprucing up oneself and lacking civic

behaviour makes achieving a *Swachh Bharat* difficult. The punch line for a clean India should be *achche se raho*...

My first meeting and conference experiences were at RSS *shakhas* and village *chaupals*. Initially, I was excited to participate in physical training exercises and listen to organisers who spoke with a knowledge of civic sense. As I grew older, I observed many *pracharaks* staying in our village home during the Emergency and later, the establishment of Saraswati *Shishu Mandir*. I was very much influenced by the RSS ideology, and during the Hindu-Muslim riots in the 1980s, I became its staunch supporter.

This admiration continued until I settled in Delhi (1984-1990) and travelled across the country, interacting with many thinkers and sharp-minded individuals. During the 1984 Delhi riots, I witnessed the burning city, walking from Nangloi to Safdarjung Enclave. This experience made me greatly admire Shri Atal Behari Vajpayee, especially during his governance from 1999-2004, when he introduced the citizen charter and broke bureaucratic shackles in business and public service.

During Manmohan Singh's regime, I observed the BJP without Atalji and noted the disrespect shown towards the great economist and good soul, Dr Singh. This led me to recall the RSS workers' behaviour from my childhood and realise the hidden agenda of transforming Hindus (a loving community) into hard core *Sanatanis*, thereby dividing them in the quest for unfettered power and dominance over their personal lives.

As a teenager, I was excited to watch the dialogues and bickering in village chaupals. However, I soon realised these gatherings lacked wisdom, justice, and foresight. They were more about power displays to dominate and subjugate the poor and weak families of the village.

Over the years, I attended numerous meetings and conferences in government, corporate, religious, and social settings. Gradually, I realised the hollowness of these gatherings due to a lack of team skills and spirit. They were merely urban versions of village *panchayats*, with decisions pre-determined and these gatherings serving as a facade for more extensive, concocted acceptability.

In my fifty plus years of experience, only two public addresses stood out: those by President Abdul Kalam and Narayan Murthy at a CA annual day. Their speeches were filled with wisdom and intellect, yet I feel disheartened that most of our fellow countrymen do not appreciate such valuable words.

From a business and economic perspective, my highest admiration goes to Dr Manmohan Singh, followed by Indira Gandhi, who uplifted the lives of the poor and underprivileged. However, these people were rarely appreciated by leaders of these sections of society, who were primarily focused on amassing wealth.

The agenda is often lost amidst futile discussions in most meetings and conferences. Personal likes and dislikes dominate, and listeners, either out of civility or fear, applaud the influential individuals present. The memento distribution and welcome style for speakers often neglect and ignore the audience entirely. With few exceptions, the primary purpose of such meetings is to win favour with the powerful and engage in wayward talks.

Religious and social conferences often empower power-hungry individuals or international agendas. Public welfare and actions to enhance public wisdom and skills are usually suppressed. Government efforts towards skill development programs often fail, filling the pockets of those with connections to fund providers.

These failures pushed me to observe closely the heavy taxation and penalisation of ordinary people and international borrowing, which ultimately burdens the common man with repayment through taxes. No conferences or meetings address the government inefficiencies and incompetence that lead to these financial burdens.

Our messed-up everyday

Numerous challenges and learning experiences have marked my journey from 1984 onwards. The pervasive culture of bullying and mediocrity in the public and private sectors has significantly hindered personal and social growth. Observing discipline and cleanliness abroad highlights the need to change our upbringing and social values to foster a more ethical, disciplined, and progressive society.

Officer training was a mixed experience, but it was enriching and highlighted the deep-seated cultural norms that resist quick fixes and require generational efforts to change. One of my colleagues even humorously nicknamed me Unfortunately Born in India (UBI), reflecting the cynicism many feel towards systemic issues like corruption and inefficiency that demand one to be exceptionally street-smart to navigate.

After sixteen years in the public sector, where I saw both waste and resource mismanagement, I transitioned to the private sector. I hoped for a more dynamic work environment but soon realised that the private sector too, is primarily driven by profit margins and often exploits natural resources without regard for broader social impact. The sector does not naturally elevate one's position; advancement often struggles against systemic inertia and requires significant personal effort.

Throughout my 28 years of professional experience, I have observed a lack of sophisticated business acumen and a dearth of macro-level strategic thinking at the top levels where they are most needed. Workplace politics and varying forms of corruption seem endemic, perpetuating cycles of inefficiency and ethical compromises. The challenge lies not only in addressing these systemic issues but also in fostering an environment where people feel valued and respected, which is essential for any meaningful, peaceful, and professional engagement.

Thus, while there have been strides in certain sectors due to individual and corporate initiatives, the broader picture reveals significant gaps in governance, corporate responsibility, and community engagement that urgently need to be addressed to truly advance the nation's socio-economic landscape.

While working in the public and private sectors, I observed a lack of individual ambition to excel beyond the standard benchmarks. Within teams, there was often a scramble to claim credit for collective efforts. This dynamic failed to generate synergy; instead, it led to a kind of energy drain where team members would subtly undermine each other. This environment is why employee costs are exorbitantly high.

Subordinates often hoped their bosses would fail, and bosses were reluctant to see their subordinates excel, perpetuating a cycle where everyone operated within a tangled web of diagonal and alternative hierarchies of communication. Despite these challenges, the success of these institutions hinged on a heavily bureaucratic system that, while yielding results, did so at an unnecessarily high cost and with frustrating slowness.

In this setting, genuine ownership of responsibilities was

rare; instead, many were quick to claim the rewards of others' hard work, adhering to the principle of 'keep doing your duty without expectation of the results because I have already sold the outcomes!' The recent examination of goof-ups and associated scams only underscores my observations about the prevailing organisational cultures.

Transitioning from employment to running my own practice, I was dismayed that the accounting profession had shifted dramatically from being a knowledge and guidance hub, safeguarding businesses from bureaucratic overreach, to merely functioning as an outsourcing service for generic tasks. Moreover, finding skilled accounts and secretarial staff has become increasingly complex, thanks to the rise of software solutions and tools like ChatGPT, which, while helpful, cannot replace the nuanced understanding a trained professional brings. This gap underscores the need for practical, hands-on training in accounts at the undergraduate level to prepare future professionals better.

Regarding client interactions, I have noticed a general reluctance to pay even reasonable fees for services, especially evident in dealings with public-sector banks and large corporations. This has led to a proliferation of intermediaries in both private and public sectors, creating layers of bureaucracy that ostensibly smooth service delivery but which actually facilitate a robust mechanism of systemic corruption.

Chartered Accountancy

The decline in the image and earnings of CAs in India over the last three decades can be attributed to the following factors:
- **Overcrowding:** Increased number of CA graduates, leading to supply exceeding demand.
- **Loss of exclusivity:** A CA certification is no longer unique, with other accounting certifications gaining recognition.
- **Perception of limited expertise:** CAs are seen as specialised in taxation and auditing, rather than as broader business advisory services.
- **Lack of technological adaptation:** Slow adoption of technology, hinders their ability to provide modern services.
- **Scandals and unethical practices:** High-profile cases damage the profession's reputation.

The factors contributing to a decline in earnings are:
- **Globalisation and automation:** Outsourcing and automation have reduced the demand for traditional CA services.
- **Competition from other professionals:** Master of

Business Administration (MBA), Company Secretary (CS), and Certified Management Accountant (CMA) professionals have begun encroaching on CA territory.
- **Commoditisation of services:** Standardised services, like auditing and taxation, have become less lucrative.
- **Regulatory changes:** Amendments to laws and regulations have reduced a CA's role.
- **Failure to adapt to the changing business landscape:** CAs are not diversifying their services to meet evolving client needs.

Some statistics related to CAs are listed below:
- India has over 3.5 lakh registered CAs (ICAI, 2022).
- Unemployment rate among CAs: 15-20 per cent (ICAI, 2020).
- Average starting salary for CAs: Rs 6-8 lakh (down from Rs 12-15 lakh in 2010).
- Median salary for experienced CAs: Rs15-25 lakh (down from Rs 30-50 lakh in 2010).

ICAI initiatives to address the decline include the following:
- Reforming curricula to incorporate emerging areas (data analytics, AI, and so on)
- Laying emphasis on continuing professional development (CPD)
- Encouraging specialisation and niche services
- Strengthening disciplinary mechanisms to maintain professionalism
- Promoting the CA profession through branding and outreach

Here are some of my suggestions for the way forward:
- Diversify services (consulting, forensic accounting, and so on)
- Develop expertise in emerging areas (blockchain, sustainability, and so on)
- Leverage technology to enhance efficiency and client services
- Foster strong networking and relationships
- Enhance soft skills and business acumen

The Chartered Accountant Act predates the Indian constitution. The very purpose of the chartered accountancy profession has lost its sheen across the world, but more so in countries highly dependent on foreign funding. Consequently, the Big Four CA firms capture the professional opportunities for CAs with more than 80 per cent value in India.

Next, the sharp decline in national basic talent due to the high dependency on technology governed by the West on one hand, and the coaching and exam cracking techniques, which are a growing menace across the education system, on the other.

The chartered accountant profession was meant to keep a financial eye on national resources and their uses by government and private people. It should have the following roles.
- Assist in maintaining proper accounts of the nation through a business and increase the individual and institutional wealth and government macros. It should have a better learning perspective than the traditional, outdated one.
- The CA exam needs to be more practice-oriented than mere rote knowledge from books.
- CA should be part of the Comptroller Auditor General's

(CAG) extended arm and not subordinate to the government, meaning it should be governed by the CAG, not by any ministry, to maintain the profession's independence.
- The ICAI should not merely be an examination body. Instead, it should adopt the role of research and development and be a recommendatory body to Parliament and the government.
- The institute should financially protect the first five professional years of CAs through a self-sustaining funding programme.
- The respective ministry should pay the CA, not the auditee, for an appointment as an auditor under any law.
- Chartered accountants are protector representatives of businesses as well as tax payers, to save against any unjust taxing or financial weakening by the government.
- The curriculum should be revised absolutely because of emerging AI and the Internet of Things (IoT), and CAs should be above tech users, like a technology enabler, to finance and accounts professions.
- The economics part in its course should be increased substantially, as technology is now in need of accountancy as a fusion of economics and accountancy to create a broader outlook in this profession.,
- Every government committee at district, commissioner, state, and national level should have a CA representative as part of the decision-making team wherever spending of money or collection of money is concerned.
- The above representation should be done from a pool created by the ICAI only through a well laid down objective process.

Listed below are some emerging areas for CAs to diversify and enhance their career prospects.
Technology-driven areas:
- Data analytics and science
- AI and Machine Learning (ML)
- Blockchain and cryptocurrency
- Cybersecurity and Information Assurance

Cloud computing and accounting software consulting and advisory services include the following:
- Financial planning and wealth management
- Risk management and internal audit
- Forensic accounting and investigation
- Sustainability and environmental accounting
- Strategy and management consulting

Specialised industries include:
- Healthcare and pharmaceutical accounting
- Financial services and banking
- Real estate and construction accounting
- eCommerce and digital business accounting

Non-profit and social impact accounting in global and international areas include:
- International Financial Reporting Standards (IFRS)
- Transfer pricing and international taxation
- Global financial management and control
- Cross-border mergers and acquisitions

International auditing and assurance soft skills and niche areas include:

- Leadership and management development
- Communication and presentation skills
- Family business and succession planning

Diversity, Equity, and Inclusion (DEI) consulting certifications to consider:
Entrepreneurship and startup accounting
- Certified Information Systems Auditor (CISA)
- Certified Analytics Professional (CAP)
- Certified Anti-Money Laundering Specialist (CAMS)
- Certified Sustainability Practitioner (CSP)

Certified Forensic Accountant (CFA) key skills to develop:
- Data analysis and interpretation
- Strategic thinking and problem-solving
- Communication and collaboration
- Technical expertise in emerging areas
- Business acumen and commercial awareness

The law is a compelling career choice for students passionate about driving social change and impacting lives. Law is not merely a profession but a powerful tool to advocate for justice, representing a voice for the voiceless, and standing up against injustice. Lawyers have the unique capability to interpret laws and transform lives through advocacy, defending the marginalised, protecting the vulnerable, and challenging entrenched systems of inequity.

However, while the law offers the potential to shape a fairer society, the reality, especially in the district courts in India, can be starkly different. Many law graduates from prestigious national law schools often gravitate towards corporate legal firms or judicial examinations, bypassing opportunities in district courts. Consequently, those who enter the district court system usually find themselves in a profession chosen not out of passion but circumstance, leading to a disillusionment reflected in the rampant unemployment among law graduates.

This disillusionment is also mirrored in the field of dentistry. Despite the high social regard for the medical profession and the allure of the doctor title, many dentists struggle with the realities of the profession post-graduation. In the wake of the mushroom growth of dental doctors, their financial prospects are sobering. Salaried dentists may earn between Rs 15,000 and Rs 70,000 per month, while those who manage private practices report earnings from Rs 80,000 to Rs 5.6 lakh per month. Yet, the distribution of earnings is uneven, with fresher and junior dentists, especially in private medical colleges, earning much less.

The challenges extend beyond individual professions to the broader educational landscape in India. For instance, engineering graduates, including those from esteemed institutions like the Indian Institute of Technology (IITs), face severe underemployment. Despite the high calibre of education, the stark reality is that one in every two engineering graduates in India are unemployed. In 2025, India will produce around 88,500 Master of Science (MS) graduates, with a significant number specialising in computer science and engineering. Yet, many of these highly trained individuals will enter a job market that is increasingly unable to absorb them due to cooling tech sectors and economic fluctuations.

The situation for IIT graduates is particularly disheartening. Recent data reveals that about 38 per cent of graduates from all twenty-three IIT campuses remain unemployed, with newer IITs experiencing even higher rates of joblessness. The traditional route of securing campus placements is proving inadequate, reflecting broader systemic issues within India's approach to higher education and job creation in tech and engineering sectors.

A tweet highlighted that around 30-40 per cent of IIT graduates either go abroad, find off-campus placements, prepare for competitive government exams like the Union Public Service Commission (UPSC), or venture into startups.

However, even moving abroad to pursue a master's degree is not an ideal solution as the situation in the US is not that rosy.

About 50,000 to 65,000 Indian students with master's degrees in computer science will graduate soon, most of whom will not land jobs.

It was noted that India sends more graduate students to the US than any other country, with around 1,66,000 students, 80 per cent of whom are pursuing master's degrees, primarily short one-to-two-year programs. These programs have become a more affordable and quicker route to potential immigration.

Many IIT graduates are turning to alternative career paths.

These educational and professional challenges highlight the need for a significant recalibration of how India trains its professionals and integrates them into the economy. While the potential for impactful careers in law, dentistry, and engineering exists, the pathways to meaningful employment are fraught with obstacles, underscoring the urgent need for systemic reforms to align education more closely with market realities and social needs.

★★★

Words of Wisdom

Readers must have heard the phrase *bade bujurg*—the elderly. One of the characteristic attributes of this stage of life is that you cannot stop yourself from sharing what you have learnt with others. Elders have always played a vital role in sharing their wisdom and experiences with younger generations. Through their life journey, they have gained valuable insights and perspectives that can guide and inspire others. In this essay, we will explore how elders share their wisdom through their experiences and the impact it has on individuals and communities.

One way in which elders share their wisdom is through storytelling. They have lived through historical events, social changes, and personal struggles to gain a unique life perspective. They can pass on their knowledge and experiences to younger generations by sharing their stories and providing valuable lessons and insights.

For example, a grandparent may share childhood stories, of growing up during a war or living through a significant social movement. These stories can help the younger generations understand the past and its impact on the present.

Another way in which elders share their wisdom is through mentorship. They can provide guidance and support to individuals who seek advice or direction. Elders have lived through various life experiences and have gained valuable wisdom that can help others navigate their paths.

For instance, a retired businessperson may mentor a young entrepreneur, sharing their knowledge and expertise to help them succeed. Elders also share their wisdom through cultural traditions and practices. They deeply understand their cultural heritage and can pass on customs, rituals, and values to younger generations. This helps to preserve cultural identity and ensures that traditional practices are continued. For example, an elder person may teach a young person how to prepare a traditional meal or perform a cultural ceremony.

Furthermore, elders share their wisdom through their presence and example. They have lived a whole life and have gained a sense of perspective and wisdom that can inspire others. Spending time with elders and observing their behaviour can be a powerful learning experience.

For instance, an elder person may demonstrate the importance of patience, kindness, and compassion, providing a role model for younger generations. The impact of elders sharing their wisdom is profound. It helps to preserve cultural heritage, provides guidance and support, and inspires personal growth. By learning from elders, individuals can gain valuable insights and perspectives that can inform their life's journey. Let me add a few paragraphs to substantiate what I have just said.

Learning without end
In the murky depths of December 1937, an unforgettable

incident unfolded during a football match between Chelsea Football Club (FC) and Charlton FC at the iconic Stamford bridge. As the fog descended, thick and impenetrable, visibility on the field dwindled to mere yards. At the 60th minute, the referee, unable to ensure the safety and fairness of play, blew his whistle to abandon the game. Yet amidst the clamour and the chaos of the crowd, one man remained oblivious to the halted play—Charlton FC's goalkeeper, Sam Bartram.

Bartram, steadfast in his duty, continued to guard his goal with intense concentration. He stood alone, peering into the dense fog, arms outstretched, waiting for a ball that never came.

For fifteen surreal minutes, he maintained his vigil until a field police officer finally reached him, delivering the news that the game had ended. His reaction was a poignant reflection: 'How sad that my friends forgot me when I was guarding their gate.'

This incident transcends the world of sports, encapsulating a more profound truth about human nature and social relationships. Like Bartram in the fog, many of us diligently guard the goals of those around us, committed to supporting and protecting our team—whether it be family, friends, or colleagues. However, when visibility dwindles, and conditions become confusing or challenging, it is not uncommon for people to feel isolated or forgotten by those they have supported.

Bartram's experience is a metaphor for when we are left in the fog of life's more obscure moments. It highlights the importance of communication, awareness, and mutual support, especially when conditions are unclear. As Bartram stood loyally at his post, many commit to their roles and responsibilities, trusting others to do the same. Yet, his story reminds us of the need to ensure that no one feels abandoned or overlooked, mainly when they are most focused on serving the group.

Goalkeeping: your best defence!

Moreover, this story also touches on the theme of resilience and the strength of character. Despite his initial sadness, Bartram's ability to voice his feelings and reflect on the situation exemplifies how one can confront and learn from even the most bewildering circumstances. It underscores the value of perseverance and the importance of maintaining one's post with diligence and honour, even when the crowd has faded and the game has paused.

In life, as in football, the fog will eventually lift. Ensuring we remain connected, supportive, and appreciative of each other's roles can make all the difference in fostering a team environment where no one feels left behind, regardless of how thick the fog gets.

Differentiating between study and learning

My lifelong observations have reinforced my belief that our educational focus is misplaced on rote learning rather than practical knowledge application. People in rural areas, often without formal education, but equipped with common sense, display more practical wisdom than urban dwellers who may boast numerous degrees yet lack basic directional sense without digital aids.

Traffic regulations, for example, are taught but not internalised, particularly by the affluent. Our educational system emphasises theoretical knowledge in geometry, physics, and biology but fails to connect these concepts with practical applications such as urban planning, culinary arts, or environmental conservation.

Driven by a passion for learning rather than just studying, I often found myself at odds with the educational status quo, which lacked coherence in curriculum design and teaching methods. This disconnect is evident in how our society values and recognises self-taught individuals like Varghese Kurien of Amul and Raj Kapoor in the film industry, who excelled due to their intuitive learning approaches.

From my experience, practical learning should be orderly and structured as exemplified by my accounts teacher, whose methodical teaching greatly enhanced my understanding of financial statements.

However, when I attempted the civil services exams, I was struck by the syllabus's emphasis on memorisation over analytical thinking, reflecting a broader issue within our governance—where procedural knowledge often supersedes practical, actionable intelligence.

Initiatives like Skill India, Clean Rivers, Swachh Bharat, and the Smart Cities project often falter, not due to a lack of resources but because of a fundamental lack of skilled macro-management and negotiation acumen among our leaders. This deficiency highlights a critical gap between academic economic theories and their practical application in governance and business, leading to systemic inefficiencies and missed opportunities.

Ultimately, despite studying management theories like those of Taylor and Fayol, I rarely saw these principles effectively implemented in my organisations. This illustrates a significant gap between academic theory and professional practice. This gap underscores the urgent need to re-evaluate our educational and professional training frameworks to better align them with the practical demands of modern governance and business.

Heavy rains have been devastating various regions from time to time, from Kashmir to Himachal, Uttarakhand, Uttar

Pradesh (UP), Bihar, Maharashtra, Gujarat, and Kerala.

This widespread destruction has engulfed roads, bridges, houses, and buildings and claimed numerous lives, leading many to label these incidents as natural calamities. This perspective is further reinforced by intellectuals and media personalities, enhancing the public's acceptance of these events as mere acts of nature.

However, similar incidents in countries like China, Canada, and the USA, although also severe, often result in less damage due to their more vital infrastructure and more robust planning. Unfortunately, our country's more significant loss is attributed to poor infrastructure, weak planning, and inappropriate development locations.

A critical gap is a lack of institutional focus on disaster research and proactive studies to mitigate natural havoc and preserve human life. This era of technological revolution, rather than advancing our preparedness, has ironically seen a rise in religious partisanship and caste-based belief systems fuelled by a lack of political acumen in post-independence politics.

Additionally, recent man-made disasters in Delhi, which claimed the lives of innocent civil services aspirants, highlight another facet of systemic failure. The civil servants who govern the country and have themselves gone through the gruelling ordeal of competitive examinations—save for a privileged few—have largely failed to improve conditions for students or address the predatory nature of the coaching industry. This is due to their ambition and a lack of visionary skills necessary to foster a better future.

Following the tragedy in Delhi, the response from both political leaders and civil servants was lacklustre, devolving into a typical blame game that has become all too common over the past two decades. This blame-shifting often results in low-level employees facing the consequences while the owners of coaching centres remain unscathed.

Turning to film and fashion, my childhood memories are filled with visits to cinema halls during the Naumi fair in my village and watching movies at reduced rates. Back then, cinema and local theatre performances at fairs, especially during Holi, provided richer insights into life than films could.

Over time, as television became more accessible, watching movies became a Sunday ritual. Our engagement with films was partly due to the abundance of leisure time, as there were fewer opportunities to pursue personal hobbies and passions.

In terms of fashion, we traditionally had clothes custom-made for festivals and weddings, which involved selecting fabrics and visiting tailors who offered limited design choices inspired by film industry trends. Over the years, this shifted towards ready-made apparel and eventually to branded and customised tailoring services like those provided by Raymond Made to Measure.

Following Hollywood, the film industry in India has seen explosive growth, becoming a major cultural force and economic powerhouse without significant government support. Despite its success, the censor board has often stifled social progress by restricting content, failing to streamline the development that could come from this powerful medium.

Similarly, the Indian fashion industry has grown at a slower pace than it might have due to a lack of governmental recognition and support. The sector has remained overshadowed by its association with the film industry and has not been celebrated as a standalone beacon of art and creativity. Influential figures like Rani Gayatri Devi have set unmatched standards in fashion. Yet, the industry suffers from poor fabric quality and a lack of innovative design that could elevate it to international standards.

In conclusion, social advance in disaster management, education, cinema, and fashion continue to be hampered by bureaucratic inertia and a lack of visionary leadership. This calls for a significant overhaul of how governance and cultural industries are managed, ensuring that progress in infrastructure, education, and artistic expression is envisioned and effectively implemented to enhance the nation's quality of life and cultural richness.

Beware of praises and poses

Temptation is a nuanced facet of the human experience, deeply intertwined with our social interactions and personal identities. One particularly compelling form of temptation is the allure of praise. Humans are inherently social creatures, and our desire for approval and recognition can drive much of our behaviour. This yearning for validation is not merely about ego; it is rooted in our evolutionary need for social cohesion and acceptance, which were historically crucial for survival.

When genuine, praise can be a powerful motivator. It reinforces behaviours that align with our personal or group goals and can enhance our self-esteem and confidence. However, the issue arises when the desire for praise becomes a driving force in our lives, overshadowing more intrinsic motivations and leading to a dependency that skews our decision-making processes. When people become overly reliant on external validation, they may make choices that do not align with their authentic selves or long-term interests.

The temptation to seek praise can lead individuals to

prioritise activities that garner immediate accolades over those that yield long-term benefits, but may not be as publicly celebrated. For example, a professional might choose a project known to attract attention and compliments from superiors rather than a more critical, behind-the-scenes task that is crucial to the company's success but less likely to be recognised.

Moreover, the seduction of praise can lead to a fragility in one's sense of self-worth. When individuals base their self-esteem on external validation, they may experience significant emotional lows when the expected praise is not forthcoming. This dependence creates a dangerous cycle in which individuals constantly seek validation to feel valued and successful.

Additionally, the desire for praise can make individuals vulnerable to manipulation. People who crave external validation might be more likely to agree with popular opinion or go along with group decisions that they privately disagree with to avoid conflict and ensure continued approval from their peers. This can stifle personal and professional growth, discouraging honest expression and risk-taking.

The antidote to the pitfalls of craving praise lies in cultivating a strong sense of intrinsic motivation and self-validation. Focusing on personal growth, setting self-directed goals, and valuing one's opinion above others can help mitigate the overpowering need for external approval. Furthermore, developing resilience through self-reflection and mindfulness practices can strengthen one's ability to appreciate constructive feedback without being unduly swayed.

While enjoying and even seeking praise is natural, maintaining a balance where such accolades enhance rather than dictate one's actions is crucial for personal integrity and genuine fulfilment. Recognising the transient nature of external validation and fostering a robust internal value system can empower individuals to navigate life's choices more authentically and resiliently.

The duality of love and hate

The duality of love and hate as two sides of the same coin is a profound concept that underscores the complex nature of human emotions and relationships. These two forces, seemingly at odds, are deeply intertwined, each capable of powerfully shaping human behaviour and social outcomes.

Historically and universally, love and hate have coexisted, influencing human interactions constructively and destructively. This dichotomy plays out in personal relationships, where deep affection can sometimes become profound disdain due to betrayal, misunderstanding, or conflict. Similarly, cultural, political, or ideological differences can ignite hatred among groups in a broader social context, yet the same differences can foster love when embraced and understood.

The notion that sometimes hatred wins and sometimes love prevails suggests a cyclical dominance where neither emotion maintains permanent supremacy. This cycle can be seen in various aspects of life. For instance, in times of war and conflict, hatred may seem to overpower love, leading to destruction and despair. However, post-conflict periods often witness a resurgence of love and reconciliation as people seek to rebuild and heal their communities.

In the realm of social justice, hatred based on discrimination and prejudice has sparked extensive suffering and division. Yet, movements driven by love and a desire for equality continue to rise against this hatred, pushing society toward greater inclusiveness and understanding.

The statement 'nothing will change' reflects an inevitable resignation from this ongoing battle between love and hatred. It suggests that as long as human nature remains the way it is, these emotions will continue to exist and influence our world. Yet, this perspective can also imply a kind of equilibrium or balance where the presence of one emotion checks the other, preventing either from becoming absolute.

However, accepting their coexistence does not mean denying the potential for change in how these emotions are expressed and managed. Education, cultural exchange, and open dialogue can shift perceptions and reduce hatred, promoting empathy and understanding. Likewise, recognising and addressing the roots of hatred—such as fear, ignorance, or scarcity—can mitigate its impact, allowing love to flourish more freely.

The interplay between love and hate is dynamic, constantly shaped by individual choices and social conditions. Each act of kindness or aggression, each policy of inclusion or exclusion, contributes to this ongoing narrative. Thus, while love and hate may always coexist, their specific expressions and the outcomes they engender are never fixed. The challenge and opportunity for humanity lie in consciously cultivating an environment where love can thrive, despite the ever-present potential for hatred.

In conclusion, the statement invites us to reflect on the persistence of these fundamental emotions and how we might tip the balance toward love, understanding, and unity, even in the face of enduring hatred.

The Tangled web of Bureaucracy

Until a few decades ago, appointments in the lower judiciary for fourth-class employees used to be at a local level. What is interesting is the way of such recruitment, as a senior judicial officer confided in me. Such appointments are no longer in vogue, but this case example gives a vivid picture of casteism pervading our mindset.

Once upon a recent past, in a district cloaked in tradition, twenty vacant positions stirred the calm of the judiciary. The local District and Sessions Judge, a figure of considerable authority and old-world charm, was charged with the daunting task of filling these roles. In this task, he sought the assistance of a younger, somewhat greener judicial officer.

Though diligent and eager, the junior officer found himself overwhelmed by the intricate dance of recruitment. After a few harried days, he returned to his mentor, his face a tableau of confusion and frustration. With a wisdom untouched by the creeping vines of corruption—so rampant in other parts of the public sector—the District Judge imparted a strategy that was as old as the hills surrounding them. 'Let us sort the wheat from the chaff,' he suggested, 'not by the strength of their character or skill, but by the lineage of their blood.'

As the applications piled high—around 400 in total—they were sorted into categories that reflected the deep social fissures of the time:

- **The Vaish void:** No applications graced this category, leaving a gap where perhaps none expected one.
- **The Rajput reservation:** A mere handful of proud Rajputs had applied, their heritage of bravery perhaps deterring them from roles perceived as subservient. The advice was clear: 'steer clear of the warrior caste; their pride does not serve us here.'
- **The Brahmin dilemma:** Brahmins, numerous in their applications, were paradoxically marked undesirable for roles involving menial tasks or domestic duties beneath their high caste. Despite their reputed culinary prowess, the notion of a Brahmin tying shoelaces was unimaginable.
- **The loyal middle castes:** The Jats, Gujjars, Yadavas, and Kurmis were warmly embraced. Their history of servitude to higher castes and their hardworking nature made them ideal candidates for the judiciary's supporting roles.
- **The caste conundrum:** Scheduled Castes (SC) had their reserved quotas, yet biases seeped through the selection process. Balmikis and Jatavs were shunned, as untouchability swept them within the communities, while Pasis and Dhobis were preferred. Their social standing was slightly higher, and their utility in chores like laundry was undeniable.
- **The Kayastha quirk:** Before strict regulations set by non-Congress regimes, Kayasthas dominated judicial appointments, favouring their kin in a subtle game of nepotism. A long list would be drawn, with SC candidates

placed at the bottom, with selections made from the top, ensuring the status quo remained undisturbed.

Special considerations for Muslims: 'They are indispensable during Hindu festivities,' the District Judge noted. With fewer religious holidays, Muslim employees were available to serve during the bustling seasons of Holi and Diwali. Moreover, the Hindu marriage season affects both the officers and the servants. Who will look after the houses without a willing service staff? And who would be better than a Muslim whose marriage dates do not coincide with those of Hindus?

The practice of 'inbreeding'—hiring relatives of existing employees—was a tactic to foster loyalty and a potential pitfall, if not managed with a deft hand. This could lead to insular groups within the staff, threatening the integrity of the workforce.

This district's judicial recruitment narrative was more than a simple tale of filling vacancies; it was a vivid illustration of the complex interplay between social values, caste dynamics, and bureaucratic practices. As echoes of the past linger in the corridors of the judiciary, the need for reform and fairness becomes ever more pressing, urging a shift towards inclusivity and integrity in public service.

Moreover, an emphasis on practical skills—driving, stitching, sewing, and cooking—began to emerge as valuable traits, heralding a slow but inevitable evolution in the criteria for public sector employment.

This tale, while rooted in tradition, hinted at the winds of change, suggesting a future where merit and ability might finally dictate one's suitability for public service.

★★★

Movers and Shakers in my Life

Writing character sketches can be daunting for even the most experienced writers. One of the primary challenges lies in creating a well-rounded and believable character in a concise and limited space. Character sketches are meant to be brief, yet they must still manage to capture the essence and complexity of a character. Another challenge is avoiding stereotypes and clichés. It is easy to fall into the trap of relying on familiar tropes or characteristics, which can result in flat and uninteresting characters. Writers must strive to create unique and nuanced characters that defy expectations.

Additionally, character sketches require a delicate balance between detail and subtlety. Too much information can overwhelm the reader, while too little can leave the character feeling one-dimensional. Writers must carefully select the most revealing and relevant details to include. Moreover, character sketches must also consider the character's motivations, backstory, and emotional depth. This can be difficult to convey in a short space, but it is essential for creating a character that feels fully realised.

Finally, character sketches must be written in a way that engages the reader and draws them into the character's world. This requires a strong narrative voice and a clear writing style. However, here in this chapter, I have attempted to write about some people who have inspired and engaged with me throughout my life. These small descriptions are not sketches but an invitation to the reader to think about how inspiration could often come from our lived experiences.

I owe many virtues—compassion, diligence, creativity, generosity, and a deep understanding of religion and intellect—to my late mother, Mrs Yashoda Devi. As the eldest daughter among her siblings, she was a pillar of strength for our immediate family, relatives, and villagers. Throughout her life, she extended help to her siblings, her father's brother's children, and any needy villagers seeking medical help. Tragically, despite her selfless service, she passed away at the age of 69 due to negligence at a renowned hospital that prioritised commercial gains over patient care. This painful experience taught me the harsh reality of trusting others' recommendations without personal discernment. Her passing remains one of my deepest regrets, as her lifetime of giving was met with ingratitude and selfishness from those she had helped. Let me add more names and thank more people.

Shri A P Agarwal

Shri A P Agarwal was an extraordinary accountancy tutor and the best teacher I have ever had during my senior secondary education. His mastery of the double-entry accounting system significantly enhanced my ability to interpret and organise financial data into coherent balance sheets. However, despite his profound impact on students like myself, he received little recognition from educational institutions or the teaching community, often viewed unfavourably by his peers due to his innovative methods and thorough teaching style.

Late Shri Yash Barry, Fellow Chartered Accountant (FCA)
During my chartered accountancy training, Shri Yash Barry, a profoundly knowledgeable and passionate professional, mentored me. Although officially under his brother's guidance, I worked closely with Shri Barry in a chaotic office environment. He instilled in me the ethic of hard work and the importance of imparting knowledge to juniors, a lesson that has served me well throughout my career. His pragmatic approach to solving complex problems and his ability to understand human nature profoundly influenced me. Sadly, his contributions were underappreciated, and his final years were marred by neglect from those he had helped, including his own family.

Late Shri Jai Singh Bhandari
Upon joining a Public Sector Unit (PSU) as a Class I officer after training, I was fortunate to work under Shri Jai Singh Bhandari in the foothills of what is now Uttarakhand. Despite a discouraging start with the Human Resources (HR) division, Shri Bhandari's transparent and ego-free approach convinced me to stay on the job. His mentorship and hospitality, along with that of his wife, were the highlights of my tenure in Mumbai and demonstrated the leadership potential that genuinely values integrity and straightforwardness. Despite his capabilities, he was often sidelined by senior management, fearful of his refusal to compromise on ethical standards, which

starkly illustrated the systemic flaws within the organisation.

Shri Anil Maheshwari: Renowned senior journalist

At a Non-Governmental Organisation (NGO) event, I first encountered Shri Anil Maheshwari, a venerable retired journalist from *Hindustan Times*. When the primary coordinator of the NGO requested that I offer him a ride home, it marked the beginning of a meaningful mentorship. During the thirty-minute car ride, I quickly realised that he was a kindred spirit from whom I could learn extensively. Our subsequent meetings deepened my understanding of the political and administrative landscapes. Under his guidance, I began documenting my experiences, transforming them into reflective essays on life and work. Shri Maheshwari's insightful commentary and sharp critique of workplace dynamics profoundly influenced my approach to writing and thinking. His expertise in identifying the mercenary nature of professional environments and correcting my misconceptions about influential figures was invaluable in shaping my perspectives.

Shri Harbans Dixit: Esteemed law scholar

Shri Harbans Dixit, a legendary figure in law education and the dean of a law faculty in Moradabad, became a mentor during my time in the city. Known to a colleague, Shri Dixit's humility and depth of knowledge were immediately apparent. His ability to host, engage, and briefly summarise discussions set a standard I aspired to emulate. Despite his significant contributions and a stint with the state's Public Service Commission, I always felt that his association with such narrowly focused initiatives somewhat constrained his potential. His leadership in organising conferences and social work impacted my approach to public service and academic excellence.

Shri B S Sidhu: Former DGP with a personal touch

Meeting Shri B S Sidhu, a former Director General of Police (DGP), enriched my understanding of humane law enforcement. Unlike many of his contemporaries, he retained a genuine, approachable demeanour, untainted by the arrogance often associated with high-ranking officials. From him, I learned practical life skills, such as parallel parking and the finer points of culinary arts. His discussions on food quality and preparation deepened my appreciation for gastronomy. Shri Sidhu's philosophy—that the intent behind one's actions defines one's character—resonated deeply with me, influencing my views on integrity and professionalism.

Shri D C Jain: IPS Officer of Integrity

Shri D C Jain, whom I first met when he was a Deputy Inspector General (DIG) of Police in the Central Bureau of Investigation (CBI), exemplified how one can wield significant power yet remain grounded. His career in bureaucracy did not diminish his humility or ability to engage with people without arrogance. His approach reinforced my belief that authentic leadership is about maintaining one's values despite the trappings of power. His ongoing service limits the details I can share, but his influence on my understanding of ethical leadership is profound.

Shri Vivek Goel: Chartered Accountant and mentor

As a young CA trainee, I was fortunate to work under

Shri Vivek Goel, a partner in the firm where I trained. His guidance during my formative years in finance was crucial. Reconnecting with him years later, I found him unchanged by success, still embodying the virtues of his youth. From him, I learned that excessive niceness could inadvertently hinder one's career and that sometimes, silence is strategic. His blend of professionalism and personal integrity inspires me to navigate my career and interpersonal relationships.

Shri Pankaj Shah: A Paragon of industrious simplicity
When we met during my official duties, Shri Pankaj Shah, a self-made industrialist from Rajasthan, impacted me profoundly. From him, I learned that wealth should not uproot one from one's origins. His principles included maintaining strict organisational control to prevent metaphorical 'rats' from causing destruction. His simplicity and hospitality, alongside with his wife's, were commendable. Shri Shah believed in realistic expectations from employees, advocating for recognising individuals' capacities rather than overburdening them. His ability to discern where actual business opportunities lay—understanding that real profit is not just reflected on balance sheets but requires a vision extending beyond immediate horizons—was inspirational.

Shri N D Sinha: Vigilance expert with a pen of justice
As the head of the vigilance department in Delhi, Shri N D Sinha was instrumental during the early days of my career in the PSU. From him, I mastered the art of drafting precise official letters and understood the intricacies and limitations of organisational vigilance systems. His personal and professional battles taught me the power of the written word

in challenging authority and advocating for justice. His ability to wield the pen effectively made him a formidable figure, capable of challenging even the most powerful with justifiable actions and a clear, strong voice.

Shri Manoj Bharti: Guide in navigating tax law

Shri Manoj Bharti, the first income tax officer I interacted with during practice, significantly shaped my professional development in tax law. His professional conduct and thorough handling of assessment proceedings provided a solid foundation for my skills in managing complex tax cases. His promotion and continued association have been a testament to the lasting impact of positive mentorship in professional settings. Shri Bharti's influence extends beyond professional guidance; he exemplifies how career-long connections can evolve into familial ties, underscoring the small-world nature of our interactions.

Late Murali Rajagopalan: A friend of inestimable value

The late Murali Rajagopalan was a colleague and a cherished friend whose qualities left an indelible mark on my life. Despite a severe accident that left him with an artificial limb, his spirit and vivacity remained unscathed. Murali's proficiency in multiple areas, from table tennis to astrology, complemented his professional acumen, making him a well-rounded and deeply admired friend and mentor. His hospitality during my visits to Chennai and Puducherry showcased his meticulous planning and deep care for friends and family, creating lasting memories. His untimely demise was a profound loss, not just personally but to all who knew him and were touched by his generous spirit and vibrant personality.

Mr Diazz: A fleeting friendship on foreign shores

Mr Diazz, whom I met in Singapore, was a remarkable individual from Columbia with an enriching perspective on life. Our brief friendship was marked by insightful conversations and shared experiences.

Mr Deo Datta

I recently had the privilege of interacting with Mr Deo Datta Sharma, a former IAS officer known for his exceptional ability to navigate complex situations with pragmatism and dynamism. His approach, which reflects a rare magnanimity, presents a refreshing side of bureaucracy—one that champions the spirit of democracy in a country plagued by poverty. Mr Sharma's style emphasises the essence of governance over rigid adherence to rules, focusing on the spirit behind these regulations to safeguard the true beneficiaries.

This experience reminded me of the theories of Herbert Simon, a renowned management theorist, particularly his decision-making model that outshines other management theories through its advocacy for timely and just decision-making. Mr Sharma is a living embodiment of the principles envisaged by the pioneers of the bureaucratic system. His ability to read between the lines and see beyond conventional bureaucratic constraints is inspiring. It is a testament to the potential of our systems and processes to act not merely as barriers but as catalysts for optimising welfare and safeguarding humanity.

Each of these individuals has significantly shaped my perspective and practices, highlighting the often-overlooked value of integrity, mentorship, and genuine human connection in both personal and professional realms. Their stories underscore the poignant reality of unrecognised contributions in a world that frequently rewards conformity over genuine merit.

The Last Word

In the last 20 years, all professions in the country have lost their sheen due to an unplanned economy in the quest for power and money. Reflecting on the past 250 years of global history, it is clear that western Christian-majority countries have been pivotal in driving progress post-eighteen hundred AD, particularly in scientific, educational, and economic arenas.

While individual contributions from Hindu and Muslim communities appear less prominent in specific international rankings, such as the top 100 scientists, the overall impact of these communities on global culture and history is significant.

Globally, 57 Islamic countries house more than 24.1per cent of the world's population, or about 1.9 billion people, but only 347 universities. In contrast, approximately 1.2 billion Hindus worldwide, about 15 per cent of the global population, are predominantly concentrated in India. This demographic distribution illustrates varying access levels to educational resources and institutions across different regions.

In the United States, home to approximately 228.1

million Christians, the educational infrastructure is robust, with around 5,300 universities and colleges. This educational wealth corresponds with a high percentage of degree-holders; about 37.7 per cent of Americans aged 25 years and older have a bachelor's degree or higher. Conversely, only 13 per cent of the adult population in India hold a university degree.

The educational attainment in Muslim-majority regions also presents challenges, with about 36 per cent Muslims having no formal schooling and only 8 per cent achieving graduate and post-graduate levels.

On the philanthropic front, religious contributions also vary. In 2014-15, Hindus in India donated over Rs15,600 crore to spiritual causes, significantly more than Muslims. However, on a per-household basis, Muslims contributed marginally more, likely influenced by the religious injunctions to give to charity. Christians, however, have the highest per-household religious contribution, reflecting broader global charitable giving trends.

Regarding wealth, notable figures such as Azim Premji from the Muslim community and no Hindus appear in the top 20 wealthiest people globally, suggesting a disparity in economic influence and visibility on the world stage.

Internationally, the United States excels in areas like the Olympics, showcasing its robust support for sports and athletic training. In contrast, other nations often lag, focusing more on regional or nationalistic pride than global competition.

The existence of about 3.6 million mosques worldwide compared to around 2 million Hindu temples highlights the extensive religious infrastructure supporting these communities globally. This analysis indicates that while Christian-majority countries, particularly the USA, have led in many aspects of social development, the contributions of Hindu and Muslim communities, both historically and in contemporary contexts, are also profound and continue to shape global civilisation in myriad ways.

Less corruption, more accountability!

We surrender about 40 per cent of our earnings to the government in the form of various taxes and fees, only for the government to spend about 20 per cent of those collections on pensions and perks for its employees. On top of this, taxpayers are often forced to pay extra service fees to government employees, who are already salaried with perks such as palatial bungalows, chauffeur driven vehicles with escorts, and servants (some official and some unofficial) paid for by our taxes, just to receive the services they are supposed to provide.

Meanwhile, some officials use the remaining funds to make outrageous purchases, such as buying a basic light bulb that costs Rs 700 in the market for Rs 6,000—and then it does not even work. They might bill taxpayers Rs 250 crores for a road that actually costs just Rs 2.5 crores to build, yet is so poorly made it resembles the cratered surface of the moon.

After all this, many government employees end up with exorbitant wealth and invest in real estate, driving prices up so high that middle-class citizens, who have been left with little, can hardly afford to live decently. Most of us pay taxes for roads that do not exist, for facilities that never materialise, and for services that are laughably inadequate.

From whatever little we save, buying anything significant is out of reach because we simply cannot afford it. Many of us labour tirelessly only to ensure that a peon or a clerk in a Regional Transport Office (RTO) or municipality can afford luxuries like a six-bedroom house, a Fortuner car, and extravagant jewels, while we are left fretting that one family illness could lead to financial ruin.

Given these circumstances, it is understandable why some choose to leave India. We pay for everything but receive nothing substantial in return; living under such conditions is not feasible for everyone.

This is all due to poor audit and review mechanisms enshrined in the economic veins of national wealth.

News that Virat Kohli and Anushka Sharma are settling in London has surfaced. That is perfectly acceptable. Choosing to stay despite better opportunities abroad is commendable, just as the decision to leave, because better resources are available elsewhere, is also a rational choice.

India, with its rich history, has unfortunately adopted a post-independence system that caters to a demographic resistant to progress—those who avoid work, thrive on oppression, and survive on freebies.

In this country, even a convicted criminal out on bail has voting rights equal to those of a law-abiding, tax-paying citizen striving to improve the nation. Our electoral concerns are dominated by identity politics and entitlements, with negligible attention to critical issues like pollution, health, or education.

Why blame the politicians when the general populace shows little concern for substantial governance? Under the current system, India's progress is stunted. I hope I am proven wrong, but reality suggests otherwise.

Interestingly, many politicians, bureaucrats, and judges ensure their offspring study, work, or settle abroad, possibly indicating their lack of faith in the system they govern.

Discussing Virat Kohli's decision to move should not be controversial; he is a private citizen and not a public official. He has earned his success and contributed significantly to our national pride. If he chooses to relocate for what he believes is a better future for his family, that decision should be respected. People often assert that if they had the means, they too would emigrate, promising to ensure a better future abroad for their next generation.

Every citizen counts
When we create some celebrities and qualified professionals then the national exchequer spends directly and indirectly a huge amount of taxpayers' money to take them up to that height. This investment does not need to return in the form of the foreign exchange they remit, rather they need to be charged for creating a liability on their passport.

The Indian populace can essentially be divided into four segments: the ultra-mega-rich who leave at the first opportunity; the ultra-rich who stay due to certain compulsions but live insulated lives mimicking western standards; the beleaguered middle class, aspiring yet constrained, who bear the brunt of the nation's inefficiencies; and the vast number of poor, largely oblivious to the struggles of the other segments and dependent on government doles.

All governments seem inclined to maintain this status quo, which is detrimental for the nation. It may be the voters' carelessness to not elect honest and talented politicians. The election commission is duty bound to raise the voters' awareness through a structured awareness programme and add a chapter to social science at the school matriculation level.

True economic growth occurs when the government

facilitates the upward mobility of its citizens—a process sorely lacking in our current system. The next five years are critical for addressing this challenge if we hope to see any real progress.

Tourism for tourists, not the mafia!

The extravagant cost of holidays in India can largely be attributed to the corruption that plagues the hospitality industry. Many luxury hotels are more about laundering ill-gotten gains than serving genuine business interests. This corruption leads to inflated prices that do not reflect economic realities, creating a market where laws of economics are blatantly ignored.

This contrasts starkly with other countries, where tourism is a crucial part of people's livelihood, ensuring competitive pricing and quality services. In India, however, the tourism sector often operates like a mafia, indifferent to whether guests are satisfied or not. The underlying issue is a systemic one, requiring sweeping reforms to ensure transparency and genuine service in the hospitality industry.

A Word of Caution

Let me share a word of caution, especially for today's generation who don't like to cook at home, but prefer to eat outside or order food home.

Remember, all that glitters is not gold and it might be easy to order food from outside, but there could be a hidden worm inside the apple you bite!

Eating food from outside, especially from non-standard kitchens, poses various health risks. Let us review some of these concerns.

Food safety concerns:
- Contamination (bacterial, viral, parasitic)
- Food handling and storage errors
- Inadequate cooking temperatures
- Cross-contamination
- Unhygienic preparation conditions

Common foodborne illnesses:
- Food poisoning (Salmonella, E. coli, Campylobacter)
- Gastroenteritis (stomach flu)
- Dysentery
- Cholera
- Typhoid fever

Non-standard kitchen risks:
- Unlicensed or unregistered vendors
- Poor sanitation and hygiene practices
- Inadequate food storage and refrigeration
- Lack of proper food handling training
- Contaminated equipment and utensils

Specific risks associated with:
- Street food: Increased risk of contamination, inadequate cooking temperatures
- Food trucks: Limited food handling and storage space
- Catering services: Potential for mass foodborne illness outbreaks
- Buffets: Self-service and communal food handling increase contamination risk
- Raw or undercooked food

Increased risk of foodborne illness: Precautions
- Choose reputable and licensed food vendors
- Check food temperature and handling practices
- Avoid raw or undercooked foods
- Wash hands frequently
- Report any food safety concerns

Symptoms of foodborne illness:
- Diarrhoea
- Vomiting
- Abdominal cramps
- Fever
- Headache

Seek medical attention if:
- Symptoms persist or worsen
- Severe vomiting or diarrhoea
- Fever above 101.5°F (38.6°C)
- Signs of dehydration
- Blood in stool or vomit

Postscript

Here is a compilation of some witty rejoinders that might leave you, my readers, with a smile on your face. Enjoy!
- Today, a man knocked on my door and asked for a small donation to the local swimming pool, so I gave him a glass of water.
- I changed my password to 'incorrect,' so whenever I forget it, the computer will say, 'Your password is incorrect.'
- Artificial intelligence is no match for natural stupidity.
- I am great at multi-tasking. I can waste time, be unproductive, and procrastinate all at once.
- If you can smile when things go wrong, you have someone in mind to blame.
- Doesn't expecting the unexpected mean that the unexpected is expected?
- Take my advice—I'm not using it.
- Hospitality is the art of making guests feel at home when you wish they were.

- Television may insult your intelligence, but nothing rubs it in like a computer.
- I bought a vacuum cleaner six months ago, and so far, it has only been gathering dust.
- Whenever someone comes up with a foolproof solution, a more talented fool comes.
- If you keep your feet firmly on the ground, you'll have trouble putting on your pants.
- A computer once beat me at chess, but it was no match for me at kickboxing.
- Ever stop to think and forget to start again?
- When I married Ms Right, I had no idea her first name was Always.
- My wife got 8 out of 10 on her driver's test. The other two guys managed to jump out of her way.
- There may be no excuse for laziness, but I'm still looking.
- Women spend more time wondering what men are thinking than men spend thinking.
- Give me ambiguity, or give me something else.
- He who laughs last thinks slowest.
- Is it wrong that only one company makes the game Monopoly?
- Women sometimes make fools of men, but most guys are the D-I-Y type.
- I would give him a nasty look, but he already had one.
- Change is inevitable, except from a vending machine.
- The grass may be greener on the other side, but you don't have to mow it.

★★★

About the Author

The author of this book is an explorer by instinct and wishes to remain ahead of the West. His childhood started in a small city, and holidaying in villages made him a nature lover. On attaining adulthood and moving to the country's capital, despite many odds, he became a CA.

Apart from forty years of work experience in both public and private sectors and also as an entrepreneur, the author has travelled extensively across India and abroad.

Additionally, he has left no opportunity to understand the contrast of life. While he loves to travel abroad for work and considers that the best places for pleasure may be found abroad, he prefers to work at the grassroot level in the most remote and poor parts of the world.

He has a passion for work and for connecting the dots with wisdom, without being swayed by any influential person, culture, or custom. His choice to be with *kaamdaar* (hard working) rather than *naamdaar* (position holder) people keeps him out of the queue to reach the top. His preference and knack for macro management keep him a little sad with the policymakers.

His religion is built around caring for women, children, and elders, and his impulse is to break all barriers and uplift the downtrodden.

He propagates for:
- Professional excellence
- Love your work
- Spend more on the best food and knowledge, not jewellery and property
    - Human capital enrichment is the only solution to all miseries
    - Learning lies more in meeting and interacting differently, making your learning in school a reality

He has also been an avid reader and analyser. He is cautious about the prevailing business disruption in the last three decades and passionate about saving youngsters from the tech onslaught.